Rebel Literacy

Rebel Literacy

Cuba's National Literacy Campaign and Critical Global Citizenship

By Mark Abendroth

Litwin Books, LLC
Duluth, Minnesota

Published by Litwin Books, LLC, 2009
PO Box 3320
Duluth, MN 55803

http://litwinbooks.com/

This book is printed on acid-free paper that meets all present ANSI standards
for archival preservation.

Library of Congress Cataloging-in-Publication Data

Abendroth, Mark.
 Rebel literacy : Cuba's national literacy campaign and critical global
citizenship / by Mark Abendroth.
   p. cm.
 Includes bibliographical references and index.
 ISBN 978-1-936117-06-2 (alk. paper)
 1. Literacy--Social aspects--Cuba. 2. Literacy programs--Cuba. 3. World
citizenship. I. Title.
 LC155.C9A34 2009
 379.2'4097291--dc22
                2009037387

Contents

Foreword: A Possible Praxis

By Peter McLaren

To the memory of Manuel Ascunce Domensch and Conrado Benitez,
Cuban literacy workers murdered by counterrevolutionary forces.

In the summer of 2000, I was invited, along with Ira Shor, to serve as an advisor for the doctoral degree program in critical pedagogy at the University of Saint Thomas (St. Paul and Minneapolis, Minnesota). I also had the good fortune to teach a summer course that same year. In those days, many of us who had been engaged since the early 1980s in the difficult task of developing critical pedagogy into a legitimate program of study in graduate schools of education dared to be optimistic about the future of the field. We were eagerly waiting to see our efforts reach fruition. Two of my former doctoral students (from Miami University of Ohio and the University of California, Los Angeles) became full-time faculty in the program at the University of St. Thomas. It was an exciting time.

I had hoped that critical pedagogy would catch fire at schools of education nationwide, and that this would lead to more doctoral programs with concentrations in critical pedagogy, and perhaps even doctoral degree programs. After all, UCLA had recruited me in 1992 to bring critical pedagogy to what is now called the Division of Urban Schooling. And colleagues of mine throughout the US were being asked to develop courses in critical pedagogy at their institutions. Perhaps critical pedagogy was coming into its own. Of course, at that time critical pedagogy (and to a certain extent today) was used as an umbrella term that covered the domains of literacy, educational philosophy and theory, ethnographic studies of schooling, language acquisition and reading, the social foundations of education, and multicultural education. So there was a lot from which to choose.

I had waited a long time for a doctoral degree in critical pedagogy to be established somewhere in the US, and when I heard
about the program at the University of St. Thomas, a prestigious
Catholic university, I was sure that more degree programs would be
in the making. Those were heady days when public enthusiasm had
been recalled from exile and was influencing the ranks of critical
educators both in the public schools and the universities. Perhaps
critical pedagogy could change the face of public schooling in the
United States, and perhaps even build a new social order where
equality and justice prevailed. Today, that enthusiasm has waned
considerably, as both public universities and schools in general have
been more completely taken over by corporate interests powered by
neoliberal capital. The critical pedagogy program at St. Thomas
exists no more. And critical pedagogy barely seems to have survived
the educational assaults of the Bush years.

*Rebel Literacy: Cuba's National Literacy Campaign and Critical Global
Citizenship* is a step-child of the Critical Pedagogy Program at St.
Thomas, which ended after only four cohorts. It's author, Mark
Abendroth, was a member of Cohort Two. As a scholar-activist,
Abendroth has produced a courageous and prescient volume that
will impact the field of critical pedagogy for years to come. Each
page of this volume will repay the reader mightily in its creative
retelling of the Cuban National Literacy Campaign—undeniably
among the world's greatest educational accomplishments of the 20th
century. Of course, this book is much more than a retelling, it is
also a rethinking of the very meaning of literacy and critical citizenship today. And for this reason it merits the attention of educators
everywhere.

As a young man, Abendroth's interest in Cuba was partially fueled by the prohibition that still exists for U.S. citizens to visit the
island. My own interest in Cuba came from a very different place.
As a Canadian, I recall billboard and magazine advertisements in-
viting Canadians to enjoy their winter holidays in the sunny island
of Cuba, and for Canadians, every potential tropical site was
viewed as a paradisiacal haven for those of us who were confined to
eight long months of winter each year. In January, 1976, at the
height of the Canadian winter (January 26 to be exact), the charis-

matic Prime Minister of Canada, Pierre Elliot Trudeau, stepped off
an Armed Forces Boeing 707 at Jose Marti airport to meet Fidel
Castro in Cuba. I was teaching at a senior public school in a village
outside of Toronto at the time, and I remember well Trudeau's
visit. Trudeau became the first leader of a NATO country to visit
Cuba since the United States instituted its vicious 1960 embargo on
the island, which the Cubans view (and rightly so) as more of a
blockade. During a speech in Cienfuegos, Trudeau exuberantly
exclaimed, "*Viva Cuba*" and "*Viva el Primer Ministro Fidel Castro!*" And
Margaret, his wife, declared Fidel to be "the sexiest man alive."
And while, as a burgeoning young leftist, I had my reservations
about Trudeau's liberal politics, I remember cheering Trudeau's
remarks in a tavern when they were televised throughout the country. At least for his three nights in Havana, Trudeau had resisted
the attempts of the United States to dictate Canada's foreign policy
(although I am sure some of the U.S. military strategists saw an advantage to having a member of NATO that close to the devil himself).

Some analysts have made the case that Fidel's Jesuit education
(grade five at the Colegio de Dolores in Santiago de Cuba and the
Colegio de Belen in Havana and Trudeau's Jesuit schooling at the
College Jean-de-Brebeuf in Montreal) has something to do with their
affinity for each other, but both their Jesuit educations occurred
prior to Vatican II and the 32nd General Congregation that followed it, although it is likely that Trudeau was at least a student at
one time of liberation theology.[1] I remember appearing in 1980 on

---

[1] Although today it appears as though the Vatican is softening its stance
against Marx, as Gregorian University professor Georg Sans in a recent
edition of *L'Osservatore Romano*, the Vatican newspaper, praised Marx,
but not without qualification, distinguishing between Marx and Marxism, calling the latter a misappropriation of Marx's theories. The publication of Sans's piece in *L'Osservatore Romano* gives it the *de facto imprima-
tur* of Pope Benedict XVI, *The Times of London* reported. See Trudy
Ring. (2009). Vatican: Marx, Wilde Not So Bad. *Advocate*. As retrieved
from: http://www.advocate.com/News/
Daily_News/2009/10/22/Vatican__Marx,_Wilde_Not_So_Bad/#

Margaret Trudeau's television show and thinking fondly about the Trudeaus' visit to Cuba, as I fielded questions about a book I had just published about my teaching experiences in a school surrounded by public housing project in North York that had suddenly become a Canadian bestseller. It was unthinkable that Fidel and Trudeau would become, in the words of former Canadian ambassador Mark Entwistle, "intellectual soulmates" at a time when all the political calculations of the era worked to prohibit such a relationship. Trudeau would not visit Fidel again until 1991, when the two men went snorkeling together, and he enjoyed three more visits with Fidel until the late 1990s. In fact, Jimmy Carter and Fidel both served as pallbearers at Trudeau's funeral in 2000. Later, it was learned that American mobster, Myer Lansky, who resented Fidel for confiscating his gambling enterprises in Havana, and who tried to have Fidel killed during Fidel's one and only formal visit to the United States, also considered assassinating Trudeau. Of course, the U.S. has repeatedly tried to assassinate Fidel, not only by recruiting mobsters John Roselli and Sam Giancana, but also through the pet project of attorney general Robert Kennedy, Operation Mongoose, which saw the recruitment of Cuban-American militants who helped to carry out counterrevolutionary operations against Cuba, which included the bombing of hospitals, the sabotage of industrial and agricultural sites (including the poisoning of Cuba's sugar crops), as well as assassinations (when president Gerald Ford issued executive order 11905, prohibiting assassination of an instrument of U.S. foreign policy, the Cuban American militants continued to terrorize the island and to this day are active, and the revelations about the Bush administration have made a mockery of executive order 11905).

Today, as in the 1970s, there is a widespread habit of mind in the United States that is founded on the most pernicious of false generalizations and accordingly associates Cuba, socialism, Fidel, and Venezuela's President Hugo Chavez with the greatest of evils. It is an era of "negative nationalism" to use the words of George Orwell. Fueled by a vehement racism, right wing pundits and politicians and large sectors of the electorate are cheering for President Obama's policies to fail, even if it means the needs of the American people will not be served. Bolstered by a bottomless pit of corporate money, media support, and right-wing officials giddy with partisan hatred, a reactionary street-protest movement is afoot, drawing at times tens of thousands of people to decry the bank bailout, the auto bailout, health care reform, the deficit and America's descent into socialism or communism, led by the 44th President of the United States. Contrast this with the spirit and vitality of the Cuban people captured in *Rebel Literacy: Cuba's National Literacy Campaign and Critical Global Citizenship* .

In *Ciudad Libertad*, an educational complex in the Playa district of Havana, there stands a small museum that commemorates Cuba's National Literacy Campaign (henceforth called the Campaign). This modest-looking white stucco structure is anything but a testament to negative nationalism; rather, it personifies what Abendroth calls "critical global citizenship"—a liberation movement designed to ensure the health and vitality of the revolution and independence from Cuba's colonial past. Few books have touched on this aspect of the Campaign, and it is to Abendroth's great credit that he makes this theme central to his work.

Before the successful completion of the Campaign, almost a million Cubans lacked basic schooling due to race, class, gender and geographic isolation (Elvy, 2007). But that was not to last long. Like the rapid brushstrokes of narrative painter Ian Francis, voluntary literacy workers took to the streets and the fields, assembling in what was to become a massive enactment of the ethical imperatives of the revolution. A total force of 308,000 volunteers worked with 707, 212 illiterate Cubans and helped them achieve a first grade level of reading and writing (to be followed in later years by the Battle for the Sixth Grade and Battle for the Ninth Grade). Cuba's overall illiteracy rate was reduced from over 20 percent, according to the last census taken before the Revolution, to 3.9 percent. (Supko, 1998).

Volunteers included popular educators (178, 000 *alfabetizadores* who taught in urban areas), workers from factories (30,000 *brigadistas obreros* who received their regular salaries while doing their literacy training), and 100,000 students between the ages of 10 and 19 who came to be known as the Conrado Benitiz Brigadistas and who carried in their knapsacks a pair of boots, two pairs of socks, an olive-green beret, a Conrado Benitez shoulder patch, a blanket, a hammock, a lantern, and copies of *Alfabeticemos* (the Campaigns official teacher's manual) and *Venceremos* (a student primer). City schools were closed down in order that students between the ages of 10 and 19, with a minimum grade six education, could leave their homes in urban centers and live with *campesino* families in the countryside. As Joanne C. Elvy (2007) puts it: "Integrated into peasant households, they worked alongside their new families by day, and then taught them how to read and write by lantern at night." This marked a profound exchange between Cubans from urban centers and those who worked in the fields. Of particular significance was the social and cultural shift of the role of women in Cuba's civic society. Over 50 percent of the volunteer teachers in the Campaign were young women, marking the first time that many of them left home and were given the opportunity to take on the same tasks as their male counterparts (Elvy, 2007). Each act of shared labor and struggle with their *campesino* compatriots, each stroke of the pen made under the sturdy lanterns carried by the *brigadistas*, became gestures of solidarity, metonymical acts that reflected in their particular victories over illiteracy, the root metaphor of revolutionary praxis: making the revolution through revolutionary acts. Eventually, red flags were hung over doorways signaling *Territorios Libres de Analfabetismo* (Territories Free of Illiteracy).

Fernández Retamar (1989 pp. 44-45) has a wonderful quotation from Che Guevara, who, in accepting the position of professor, *honoris causa*, at the School of Pedagogy, University of Las Villas, in December, 1959, proposed to the university professors and students the kind of transformation that all of them would have to undergo in order to be considered truly useful to the construction of a socialist society. And in Marti's terms, this meant moving from the European University to the University of the Americas:

> I would never think of demanding that the distinguished professors or the students presently associated with the University of Las Villas perform the miracle of admitting to the university the masses of workers and peasants. The road here is long; it is a process all of you have lived through, one entailing many years of

preparatory study. What I do ask, based on my own limited experience as a revolutionary and rebel commandante, is that the present students of the University of Las Villas understand that study is the patrimony of no one and that the place of study where you carry out your work is the patrimony of no one – it belongs to all the people of Cuba, and it must be extended to the people or the people will seize it. And I hope - because I began the whole series of ups and downs in my career as a university student, as a member of the middle class, as a doctor with middle-class perspectives and the same youthful aspirations that you must have, and because I am convinced of the overwhelming necessity of the revolution and the infinite justice of the people's cause – I would hope for those reasons that you, today proprietors of the university, will extend it to the people. I do not say this as a threat, so as to avoid its being taken over by them tomorrow. I say it simply because it would be one more among so many beautiful examples in Cuba today: that the proprietors of the Central University of Las Villas, the students, offer it to the people through their revolutionary government. And to the distinguished professors, my colleagues, I have to say something similar: become black, mulatto, a worker, a peasant; go down among the people, respond to the people, that is, to all the necessities of all of Cuba. When this is accomplished, no one will be the loser, we all will have gained, and Cuba can then continue its march toward the future with a more vigorous step, and you will need to include in your cloister this doctor, commandante, bank president, and today professor of pedagogy who now takes leave of you.

Shortly after his speech at the University of Las Villas, Ché spoke to the problem of illiteracy in Cuba:

There are more illiterates in Cuba today than there were twenty-five years ago, because the whole government educational policy has consisted of embezzling and of building a few insignificant schools at the more central crossroads of the country. Our task is another, *compañeros*; we can rely on the people as a whole. We do not have to go beg for votes by building an insignificant school next to a highway. We are going to put that school where it is needed, where it fulfills its educational function for the people's benefit. (cited in Supko, 1998).

These views voiced by Che illustrate the attitude that animated the Campaign and made it so successful. The Campaign was able to develop appropriate strategies and tactics that were part of both methodological and doctrinal fronts. Paulo Freire (1985, p. 17) makes a distinction between strategy and tactics:

> Strategy is, as I understand it, the space in which I have my dream, my political dream, the objective of my life. It does not mean that my dream stays eternally, permanently, like it was at the beginning. Tactics, on the other hand are different. They concretize the dream. We have to be very consistent between tactics and strategy. It means that I cannot have tactics of a rightist man in order to concretize the dreams of a leftist....I remember Guevara said 'no contradictions between the means and the objectives'.

Not only did the Campaign have a strategy—building socialism—it created pedagogical tactics that were consistent with that strategy. The Campaign also benefitted from Anibal Ponce's stress on creating both a methodological front—emphasizing collective work instead of the usual bourgeois call for increasing individual freedoms—and a doctrinal front—creating a curriculum that serves the interests of workers and *campesinos*. The methodological front was also evident in the emphasis placed on collaboration among all Cuban citizens—white, black, male, female. And the doctrinal front was further revealed in the creation of a curriculum that explored colonial oppression and understanding the transformative projects of the revolution. Of course, the Campaign also benefitted from the insights of Sandino, Mello, Mao, Mariategui, Marti and others.

At this present historical conjuncture, when we are living in the bowels of a crisis of capitalism, the likes of which we have not seen since the Great Depression, when increasing numbers of people are being thrown out of their homes and denied medical assistance because of a lack of health insurance, it is not as surprising as it is disconcerting that some educationalists, such as William F. Pinar (2009), are attacking proponents of critical pedagogy for not acknowledging the lineaments of subjectivity or paying insufficient attention to theorizing the "I" in their work, and for focusing too much on social structure and the role that education plays in the

reproduction of inequality and injustice. Discussions of the importance of Che or Freire are ridiculed by Pinar as attempts by critical
educators to sell commodified "metasubjects" to students, creating
a "doomed defiance" and an "impossible praxis." Having ignored
the search for a self-critical subjectivity (apparently Pinar's own
mission), in its eternal repetition of the same, he argues that critical
scholarship (that is critical scholarship *sans* Pinar) has produced "no
new insight, no accumulated knowledge or intellectual advance-
ment" since 1968, despite the offspring of the *soixante-huitards* in
Paris, Berlin, Grosvenor Square, or Prague to carry on the struggle.
Pinar's aqueous clarion call to move "beyond" the antediluvian
categories of reproduction and resistance and to embrace Pinar's
sanctified "I," just at a time when the work of critical educators,
especially Marxist educators, is increasing in relevance because of
the explanatory potential of historical materialist critique to explain
the *entrañas* or *tripas* of the current crisis of capitalism, to reveal the
limitations of poststructuralism in its criticisms of Marxism as "de-
terministic" and to put class analysis back on the educational
agenda.[2]

Inspired by the examples of Fidel, Che, and others, the hundreds of thousands of volunteers in the Cuban National Literacy
Campaign were able to create a praxis, a possible praxis, without
the benefit of Delphic utterances on the importance of self-critical
subjectivity made by Pinar as he squats in Foucault's metaphysical
brianpan.[3] Nor does Venezuela's ongoing Bolivarian revolution
seem hindered by a lack of poststructuralist insight *qua* Pinar.[4]

---

[2] Those educationalists (including poststructuralists) who accuse Marx
of being a "determinist" confuse *determination* with *determinism*. Marx's
Capital does not present a fatalistic theory that all peoples must or will
endure. It presents an image of the trajectory of the logic of capital (Peter Hudis, personal communication).

[3] Thanks to Joel Spring for alerting me to the Pinar critique.

[4] This is not to say that the struggle for self-critical subjectivity is unim-
portant. What is problematic is the attempt by educationalists such as
Pinar to denigrate the accomplishments of Marxist critique (due in
large part to their superficial characterization of Marxism) in their attempt to reinsert "culture" and "subjectivity" at the center of critical

Rebel Literacy: Cuba's National Literacy Campaign and Critical Global Citizenship is a shining example of the work that needs to be undertaken today. Abendroth links this work to the foundations of critical global citizenship that can be found in critical race theory, the historical connections between indigenous struggles for sovereignty and emancipation of the African Diaspora, international feminism, and a progressive critique of transnational capitalism. It can also be seen in international struggles for socialism, efforts of those developing a de-colonizing pedagogy as well as anti-imperialist struggles worldwide.

Major accomplishments, such as the new "Organic Education Law" (see Suggett, 2009) which Venezuela's National Assembly passed unanimously shortly after midnight on August 14th following an extended legislative session, could not have been possible without the triumph of Cuba's National Literacy Campaign. Those fierce opponents of Chavez who claim the education law is unconstitutional, anti-democratic, politicizes the classroom, threatens the family and religion, and will allow the state to take children away from their parents for the purposes of political indoctrination, are reminiscent of the Cuban counterrevolutionaries who were against the Campaign. Of course, these condemnations by the Venezolano right-wing are part of a well-orchestrated campaign, which, like in the case of Cuba's Campaign, is funded by Washington. But the Organic Education Act is important in that the state has the responsibility to ensure that all citizens have a high quality education, free of charge, from childhood through the undergraduate university level (Suggett, 2009). The concept of the "Educator State" (*Estado Docente*) is introduced in Article 5, which asserts that the state must guarantee education "as a universal human right and a fundamental, inalienable, non-renounceable social duty, and a public service... governed by the principles of integrality, cooperation, solidarity, attentiveness, and co-responsibility" (Suggett, 2009). The law also requires "progressive annual growth" in education spend-

---

educational work. See Dave Hill, Peter McLaren, Mike Cole and Glenn Rikowski, eds., *Marxism Against Postmodernism in Educational Theory*, Lanham, Maryland, Lexington Books, 2003.

ing as a percentage of GDP. Article 6 lists nearly fifty aspects of the education system of which the state is in charge, including educational infrastructure, curriculum, and other administrative tasks, as well as specific duties that exemplify the principles of the education system established in Article 3. One of the key principles, in my view, advocates "equality among all citizens without discrimination of any kind." In fact, this new law mandates "equality of conditions and opportunities," as well as "gender equity," "access to the educational system for people with disabilities or educational needs," and the extension of educational facilities to rural and poor areas. Spanish is listed as the official language of the education system, "except in the instances of intercultural bilingual indigenous education, in which the official and equal use of their [native] language and Spanish shall be guaranteed." In addition to promoting "the exchange of social and artistic knowledge, theories, practices, and experiences," the law sanctions "popular and ancestral knowledge, which strengthen the identity of our Latin American, Caribbean, indigenous, and afro-descendent peoples." Finally, Article 10 specifically prohibits speech and propaganda that promote hate and violence in classrooms or in the context of educational settings, including the news media. Article 3 also stresses a recurrent theme: that of "participatory democracy." This is clearly important, and you can hear this echo throughout the new education act. Article 15 is perhaps the most controversial in the eyes of Chavez's opponents because it stipulates that one of the basic purposes of education is "to develop a new political culture based on protagonist participation and the strengthening of popular power, the democratization of knowledge, and the promotion of the school as a space for the formation of citizenship and community participation, for the reconstruction of the public spirit." Yet there are plenty of references to the importance of "learning to peacefully coexist," learning to learn and teach simultaneously, "valuing the common good," the necessity for education to be "integral" as opposed to highly specialized. The act emphasizes a "respect for diversity," and the importance of life-long learning. The legal definition of the educational community has been significantly broadened to include families, community organizations, and wage laborers in addition to the formal educational workers. Article 20 states, "The educational community will be composed of all the fathers, mothers, representatives, students, teachers, administrative workers, and laborers of the educational institution... spokespersons of the different community organizations linked to the educational centers and institutions will also be able to form part of the educational community." This new educational community is described in the article as "a democratic space of social-communitarian, organized, participatory, cooperative, protagonist, and solidarity-oriented character." The Organic Education Act also deals with questions of labor rights, job security and benefits, and training in "liberatory work." Article 15 asserts that the educational system must "develop the creative potential of each human being for the full realization of his or her personality and citizenship, based on the ethical value of liberatory work and active participation." (Suggett, 2009) There is also a stress on human rights and free speech. The law also maintains that education should encourage an end to nuclear weapons in the world, that it should fight racism and develop with students an ecological consciousness to preserve biodiversity and social diversity. The Organic Education Act is a profound historical achievement, and resistance to this act is sure to animate Venezuelan politics for years to come. The historical struggles that have, and continue to take place in Cuba, and now Venezuela, are indeed heartening, and give us reason for optimism.

Rebel Literacy: Cuba's National Literacy Campaign and Critical Global Citizenship demythologizes the Cuba that US capitalists have constructed for public consumption through the hegemonizing powers of the corporate media; not only does it show the vibrant and courageous history of Cuba's march towards socialism and participatory democracy, it makes a profound case for high-quality education as a international human right. *Rebel Literacy: Cuba's National Literacy Campaign and Critical Global Citizenship* needs to be read by teachers, teacher educators, students, administrators, and educational policy makers. In highlighting the sense of community and egalitarianism as revolutionary values that still intrinsically animate youth culture in Cuba, Abendroth not only advances a powerful critique of US educational imperatives that link educational performance with individualism, earning capacity and the ability to consume, but also makes a powerful case for critical pedagogy and popular education as a transnational social movement—in fact, a way to make people's power a reality, a way of life.

Peter McLaren
Los Angeles

References

Elvy, Joanne C. (2007). Women in the Cuban Literacy Campaign. *Literacies*, no. 7 (Fall), as retrieved from http://www.literacyjournal.ca/literacies/7-2007/pdf/elvy.pdf

Freire, Paulo. (1985). "Dialogue is Not a Chaste Event." Comments by Paulo Freire on Issues in Participatory Research. Center for International Education, School of Education, Hills House South, University of Massachusetts, Amherst. Compiled by Paul Jurmo.

Retamar, Roberto Fernandez. (1989). *Caliban and Other Essays.* Minneapolis, Minnesota: University of Minnesota Press.

Pinar, William F. (2009). The Unaddressed "I" of Ideology Critique. Power and Education, vol. 1, no. 2, as retrieved from http://dx.doi.org/10.2304/power.2009.1.2.189

Suggett, James. (2009). Venezuelan Education Law: Socialist Indoctrination or Liberatory Education? *Venezuelanalysis.com* (August 21). *As retrieved from:* http://www.venezuelanalysis.com/analysis/4734

Supko, Ruth. (1998). Perspectives of the Cuban National Literacy Campaign. Paper prepared Prepared for delivery at the 1998 meeting of the Latin American Studies Association, Palmer House Hilton Hotel, Chicago, Illinois, September 24-26, 1998.

Acknowledgements

There are many people who helped to make this book possible. I want to begin by thanking my parents, who consistently encouraged me to ask questions and to make my own path in life. They gave me a foundation for becoming a dreamer and worker in joining struggles for a better world.

I need to thank Rory Litwin for his interest in publishing my work and for recommending readings on the dissertation-to-book process. I am also grateful to my friends Barbara Smith and Brendan Obern for feedback on my early drafts.

I thank again the three members of my dissertation committee. John Holst, my dedicated committee chair, was the one who designed and instructed the University of St. Thomas' introductory course on education in Cuba. It was during that 11-day trip to Havana that I first learned about the National Literacy Campaign. Felipe de J. Pérez Cruz, the sole Cuban of my committee, unselfishly gave his time to connect me with people and places for my literature review and data collection. His warm welcome and enthusiastic support helped immensely to make my work in Cuba a pleasure. August Nimtz, Jr. provided important guidance as well for refining my theoretical approach. As a scholar and activist, he embodies solidarity with the people of Cuba and with global struggles for justice.

I thank the entire faculty who worked in the Critical Pedagogy program at St. Thomas. It was a powerful program, and I am saddened that it ended after only four cohorts. I thank my fellow members of Cohort Two. We shared many challenges and joys while working to reach greater understandings of how education can make a difference in our troubled world.

I thank Mary Walsh, librarian in charge of interlibrary loans at Adams State College, where I taught from 2006 to 2009. She showed great patience with my numerous requests.

Finally, I thank all the Cuban people who extended a generous welcome to me. There are far too many to name here, but I must highlight some names. Julio Macías Macías, my interpreter, made it

possible for my interviews and focus groups to involve real communication. My Spanish did improve but never to the level necessary
for working without Julio's help. I also need to thank Dolores
Guerra and Luis Montes de Oca, friends of Felipe de J. Pérez Cruz
who allowed me to rent room and board in their Havana apartment at a rate that I could afford. Their hospitality was incredibly
generous. I have missed the friends I made in Cuba, and I join with
others in the US to work toward bringing an end to my government's shameful policies of the travel ban and the economic blockade.

Preface

I cannot remember how old I was when I first learned that my government prohibited me and all US citizens from traveling to Cuba. The restriction only made me more inclined to want to visit Cuba and to see for myself what life was like there. An opportunity to visit legally came at the end of 2001, when I joined nine other graduate students and a professor of education on a trip that involved an introductory course on education in Cuba. On one of the 11 days there, we went to the Museum of the National Literacy Campaign in Havana. The brief introduction to the 1961 Campaign left me wanting to learn more, and I ended up returning to Cuba during my next two summer vacations from teaching to work on a dissertation about the Campaign and its content elements of civic education and global citizenship. This book is a reworking of that research.

The Campaign was an amazing accomplishment that resulted from vision, mass participation, and sacrifice. Its importance cannot be understood without studying its antecedents and its legacy, and I address those in these pages. I also devote an entire chapter to testimonies of Campaign participants who volunteered their time for my interviews and focus groups in 2003. They are ordinary Cuban citizens who helped to transform their nation in the Year of Education with various roles. The trained instructors were mostly urban adolescents, and their students and hosts were mostly rural adults who had never before learned to read or write. Professional educators coached the young instructors, and many others worked behind the scenes in administration, transportation, and other functions.

A theme that emerged in my interpretation of the Campaign is that of 'critical global citizenship', a phrase that already existed. In my work here the word 'critical' refers to an orientation that questions the status quo and the assumptions supporting it, that resists oppression, and that struggles for creating new realities in affirmation of human dignity. I am taking it from the critical pedagogy that has been a work in progress since Paulo Freire wrote *Pedagogy of the oppressed*, first published in 1970. The Cuban Revolution that triumphed in 1959 was a critical departure from the US-dominated neocolonial status quo that had defined the republic's existence since 1899. The Campaign was a resulting struggle to end the oppressive illiteracy that colonialism and neocolonialism had perpetuated. I'm using the word 'global' to emphasize Cuba's nationalism of emancipation and internationalism of solidarity. The nation's hard-fought struggle for sovereignty has led to its empathetic identity with the challenges and potential of all of Latin America and the 'Third World', and there are many actions that have been expressions of this global identity. Finally, the word 'citizenship' here involves a sense of history with regard to one's idea of belonging in the movement toward a greater love for humanity. The critical global citizen, then, is one who finds meaning and purpose in engaging with the struggles that unite people against oppression and for justice anywhere and everywhere. Of course, no human being can be devoted to all causes around the planet, but anyone can become more aware of the interconnectedness of all places in our globalized world. Such awareness can move a person to change and to become an agent of change.

Cuba is neither heaven nor hell. It is a small nation with a big presence in the world, trying to be its own master in its destiny. Its socialist project has endured nearly 50 years of a harsh economic embargo, which Cubans call a blockade and an economic war, from the US. Another test of the Cuban Revolution has been the 'Special Period' of economic hardship following the collapse of the Soviet Union along with its favorable trade relations extended to Cuba. Despite the economic struggles, the Cuban government has continued to provide universal health care, free education through graduate school, and guaranteed social security for its citizens. The National Literacy Campaign gave the Revolution an educational foundation from which to build a new citizenship, and the result has been a socialism that is uniquely Cuban and a commitment to re-invent it with mass participation from ordinary citizens. Cuba does not have a liberal democracy created in the image of the United States. Citizens directly nominate and elect legislative representatives only at the municipal level while voting to confirm candidates selected within the government at the provincial and national levels. Those municipal elections, though, are free of the influences of money and sound-bite advertisements. People nominate and vote based on candidates' reputations for having served the community. The Communist Party of Cuba stays out of electoral affairs, and candidates are neither required nor pressured to be members.

I visited Cuba and studied its National Literacy Campaign as a curious doctoral student from *Yankeelandia*. I did not know how Cubans would receive me, but I found immediately that people treated me with kindness and that those who participated in the Campaign were eager to tell me their stories and their perspectives. The Cuban member of my dissertation committee, Dr. Felipe de J. Pérez Cruz, generously gave his time in helping me find a few interviewees, and those few led us to more until I had about 100 testimonies. Pérez Cruz suggested that I try to find Cuban emigrants in Miami who had participated in the Campaign in order to receive their perspectives. As a new assistant professor of education in 2006, I tried to set up the possibility for a follow-up study there, but none of the several scholarly and cultural organizations that I contacted returned my calls.

The Cuban Revolution is a complex human process, and I feel humbled and honored to have been able to study its educational foundation. My hope is that this book will be helpful as people seek diverse sources in order to reach a deeper understanding of Cuba's place in the world. My search for this deeper understanding continues.

1. Introduction: Why Revisit Cuba's National Literacy Campaign Now?

As our world changes rapidly in what has been called globalization, the concept of global citizenship has emerged. United States citizens, if we come to realize that our nation has unprecedented power among the world's nations, have different interpretations of global citizenship. We can be paternalistic or even chauvinistic in our views of global citizenship, or we can reach a different understanding of the concept through a critical lens on power and domination. Cuban citizens, as they have learned of their historic and current struggles for national sovereignty, have a perspective on global citizenship that is quite different from that of US citizens. Cuba experienced a prolonged colonialism under Spain and is struggling to break free from neocolonialism under the US. As citizens of Cuba, the US, and all countries try to identify their orientations toward global citizenship, there is a need for what has been called critical global citizenship. Viewing globalization through a critical lens, people can become critical global citizens with priorities for advancing empathy, solidarity, and social justice in the world. Critical global citizens study the history of power and domination while seeking a vision for a greater humanity, and the history of Cuba through a lens of critical global citizenship, with a focus on the National Literacy Campaign of 1961, provides an important example of a struggle filled with hope.

Cuba represents an important turning point in world history. It became the first nation in Latin America to chart and sustain its own course politically, economically, and socially despite the will of its powerful neighbor to the north. Other countries in Latin America had experienced nationalist movements trying to do the same – most notably Mexico, Nicaragua, and Guatemala. When the US succeeded in orchestrating the military overthrow of the democratically elected presidency of Jacobo Arbenz Guzmán in Guatemala in 1954, Argentine doctor Ernesto "Ché" Guevara became convinced of the need to join Fidel Castro's small revolutionary organi-

zation stationed in Mexico with plans to transform Cuba or die trying (Guevara, 1968). The resulting Cuban Revolution that triumphed in 1959 continues to trouble the US government today,
nearly twenty years after the end of the Cold War.

The Revolution triumphed after two years of grueling guerrilla
warfare. The new revolutionary government faced the challenges of
implementing the reforms spelled out in Castro's famous speech
titled *History will absolve me*, delivered to a court in 1953 before his
conviction and imprisonment for his leadership in the attack on the
Moncada barracks. A redistribution of land was the first priority.
Lands held by wealthy national and international owners became
the property of agricultural cooperatives and the state. Among
other immediate concerns was the problem of illiteracy. The survival of the Revolution depended on keeping the hearts and minds
of Cuban citizens satisfied. A goal to eliminate illiteracy joined the
task of developing a new citizenship for Cubans.

Cuba, like many Latin American countries, inherited from colonialism a tradition in which education was a privilege rather than
a human right. A census of 1953, Cuba's last before 1959, identified
23.6 percent of the nation's people as illiterate. The National Literacy Campaign of 1961 lowered that figure, as confirmed by a
United Nations study, to 3.9 percent (Lorenzetto & Neys, 1965).
How that transformation occurred is a subject of rare mass participation. Since many teachers opposed to the Revolution had left for
the US, the task of teaching the mostly rural illiterate people fell to
the mostly urban literate adolescents. Schools closed to enable
teachers to coach the young volunteer instructors, who needed official parental permission in order to leave their homes for a teaching
assignment. Each willing rural family in need of teaching hosted a
young teacher in its home. By sharing in the work, the guest
learned quickly about the hardships of rural poverty and the hard
work of living off of the land. In return, the young visitor used the
training and the materials of the Campaign to bring reading and
writing into the lives of the host family.

Before and during the Campaign's initial mass push, a violent
opposition tested the will of Cubans. The Campaign was in a trial
stage in January of 1961 when counter-revolutionary terrorists bru-

tally murdered a young literacy instructor in a rural zone away from his home. Conrado Benítez was 18 years old, and he became a martyr. The youth who later would leave their homes to teach in rural zones became known as Conrado Benítez *brigadistas*. As the nation began the full force of its literacy work in April, the US attacked air bases in Cuba. Two days after those bombings, the famous US invasion at Bay of Pigs, known as Playa Girón in Cuba, failed to mobilize Cubans against the revolutionary government and faced defeat in three days.

These episodes of counterrevolutionary violence and others that followed only emboldened Cubans in their resolve to accomplish the goal of eliminating illiteracy within a year. By summer leaders were concerned that the work was not on pace for a December completion, and they recruited literate workers to teach illiterate co-workers while increasing the drive to mobilize participation of all potential teachers and all illiterate citizens in neighborhoods throughout the nation. The early November murder of another young instructor, Manuel Ascunce, brought another martyr to the Campaign. Municipalities, one by one, declared their completion in *alfabetizando* [making literate] all of its residents who had been identified as illiterate. The culminating assignment for the newly literate person was to write a letter to Castro, and approximately 707,000 such letters are in the Museum of the Literacy Campaign in Havana. On December 22, 1961, Cubans celebrated the end of the successful Campaign in Havana, and the young instructors were home for Christmas.

The work of 1961 was only a beginning. A follow-up program encouraged newly literate people to continue their education to at least a sixth-grade level. The government built schools in rural zones where there had not been any and enforced compulsory education for all Cuban youth through the ninth grade. Subsidies have provided free university education through graduate levels for all citizens who are academically prepared. Education, along with land reform and health care, has become one of the pillars of the Revolution.

The effects of Cuba's revolutionary education project have been international as well. Many Cubans fought in Angola's civil

war in the 1970s to defeat the UNITA rebels, who were allied with
Western nations, including the US, and with the racist apartheid
regime of South Africa. Cuban educators supported Nicaragua's
literacy campaign in the early 1980s. In 2006, UNESCO (United
Nations Educational, Scientific and Cultural Organization)
awarded one of two King Sejong Literacy Prizes to Cuba's Latin
American and Caribbean Pedagogical Institute (IPLAC) for its in-
novative work in literacy campaigns of 15 countries, including
Venezuela and Ecuador. Cuban medical doctors have worked in
many countries with severe shortages of health professionals. Youth
from Latin America and the US who are academically qualified for
medical school but lack money for the expenses have gone to Cuba
for their advanced studies. Clearly, Cuban educators have promoted a critical global citizenship with powerful results.

This theme of critical global citizenship is my focus in this book
about Cuba's National Literacy Campaign. It is a central theme in
all phases of Cuba's post-Columbian history—colonial, neocolonial,
and revolutionary. Cubans who struggled for independence against
imperialist Spain identified with the critical global citizenship of
neighboring Latin American colonies in various phases of the same
struggle. After gaining independence from Spain, Cubans struggled
for a new nationalism, identifying with José Marti's critical global
citizenship that could foresee US imperialism as Cuba's second
challenge for true independence. Since the 1959 triumph of the
Revolution, Cuba has struggled to defend its independence against
the US military attacks of 1961 and an ongoing economic blockade
by the US. A strong identification with critical global citizenship, as
I will argue, is central to Cuba's will to sustain its independence.

Critical global citizenship and Cuban history

It is common knowledge that the world today is becoming increasingly globalized. Advances in global transportation have
reached a plateau with the airplane, but global communications are
bringing rapid changes to the way people live. As the Internet
makes all kinds and qualities of information easily available, the
need for critical thinking skills becomes greater. At stake is the in-

creased potential for either socialization into the status quo or literacy for change agency.

Global citizenship is a phrase that has become cliché, and I need to contrast it with my interpretation of critical global citizenship. Any transnational corporation that searches the world for the cheapest labor and absent health and environmental standards can misrepresent itself as an entity that practices global citizenship. Any military conquest for narrow economic and political interests can be misrepresented as an altruistic "operation" for "freedom" in the name of global citizenship. A critical analysis is necessary for exposing contradictions and deceptions behind the label.

Critical global citizenship is a relatively new phrase with different interpretations of *critical*. Some educators, when connecting global citizenship with critical thinking, now refer to critical global citizenship (White & Openshaw, 2004). This is important and powerful only if the critical thinking leads to action. Only by learning to become an agent of change can someone become a critical global citizen, and this involves a long process of effort and focus. The media, schools, governments, and corporations lead people to believe that globalization is inevitable, and perhaps it is. What is not inevitable, though, is the way that globalization plays out. There are real conflicts over this, and people need to be empowered with literacy for critical global citizenship in order to participate democratically in debates and problem-solving efforts.

The current state of globalization is alarmingly undemocratic. The United Nations is a powerless entity for making global policies because each of the five permanent nations in the Security Council has complete veto power. One of those five is the US, the most powerful nation economically, politically, and, especially, militarily in the history of the world. Key global advances affecting war and peace, prosperity and hunger, diseases and remedies – all can be subverted unilaterally by the leaders of a single nation. There seems to be little outcry about this, but that is due to the partnership between the beneficiaries of this world order and the global media that serve their interests.

An important example of the undemocratic nature of this so-called world order is the annual vote by all member nations of the

UN to denounce the US embargo on trade with Cuba. The vote
has been overwhelmingly in favor of ending the embargo every
year since it was first counted in 1992. The most recent vote as of
this writing, in 2008, was 185 to 3 with two abstentions. The votes
against ending the embargo were by the US, Israel, and Palau, and
the abstentions were by Micronesia and the Marshall Islands. Many
Cubans call the US policy a blockade instead of an embargo, and
this is more accurate. The US has an enormous share in the volume
of global trade, and it can and does stop transactions with any
company from another country that also does business with Cuba.
Many such companies avoid this risk and simply stop shipments to
Cuba. As a result, Cuba has undergone many shortages in important supplies, including foods and medicines, since the 1960 advent
of the blockade. The Cuban government regularly and openly calls
this blockade an act of economic warfare.

This annual UN vote against the blockade appears briefly in
mainstream US newspapers for a single day and disappears for another year. Such articles quote responses from US and Cuban government officials. Typically, the US official denounces the Cuban
government as a tyranny or a dictatorship. Demonizing Fidel Castro and now his brother Raúl, current President since Fidel's health
problems forced him to step down in 2006, has been the simple
strategy of the US government for discrediting the Cuban Revolution. Republicans and Democrats share in this strategy because the
reward is the votes of Cuban immigrants in Florida, an important
swing state as the 2000 presidential election attests.

At the heart of this example of the blockade lies the fact that
one cannot understand Cuba without understanding its place in the
world, especially in its relations with the US. Cuba is much unlike
an island in the sense that it was engulfed by political and economic
penetrations first from Spain and then from the US. Cubans have
resisted this outside domination, and their struggle continues. There
is a long history of US actions and expressions in the interest of
controlling Latin America, going back officially to the Monroe Doctrine of 1823. The US conquest of a third of Mexico in the 1840s
demonstrated the willingness of the US government to use force in
order to expand or maintain its control, and many examples of US

aggression in Latin America have followed since then. Cuba won its second war for independence from Spain in 1898 only to face a US military occupation that became an official and long-term US policy with the Platt Amendment of 1902. What followed in Cuba was a long series of dictatorships that were, to different degrees, friendly with US political and economic interests. Much of Cuban literature calls this period from 1898 to 1958 the 'pseudo-republic'. Fulgencio Batista came to power through a coup d'état twice – in 1934 as military strongman and in 1952 as self-declared president – to replace administrations that the US government deemed too leftist, and Presidents Roosevelt and Eisenhower, respectively, gave full support to this loyal intimidator. Batista's second dictatorship, though, met an uprising that could not be contained, beginning with the attack on the Moncada Barracks in 1953 with Castro's leadership.

This uprising culminated in the guerrilla warfare that began with only 82 men led by Castro aboard a small boat named Granma, leaving Mexico on November 25, 1956, and landing on December 2 in Cuba. This small group grew into a large Revolutionary Army as landless peasants joined. As mountainous zones of the Oriente Province became liberated, Che Guevara led efforts to set up schools where there never had been any. The US supported Batista's army from the Guantánamo base with weapons and fuel for planes, but the Revolutionary Army prevailed by late 1958 through great sacrifice and through support from the revolutionary underground in cities. The Revolution celebrated its triumph on January 1, 1959, as Batista fled the island.

Cubans, whether they have identified themselves with the Revolution or against it, cannot speak of national identity at length without addressing the power of the US. Citizens of the US, on the other hand, are likely not to think of Cuba as they describe their national identity, especially since the so-called War on Terror has dominated international news. As with national identity, the concept of global citizenship is affected by perspective. Critical global citizenship necessarily looks at all perspectives, assumptions, interests, and contradictions. That is not to say that it is lost in moral relativism. Critical global citizens seek clarity by analyzing facts, propaganda, and ideology. Their conclusions often compel them to rethink their values and to take action for defending a social justice or confronting a social injustice. No great and good change has ever occurred without a vision of hope and a commitment to action.

Globalization, neoliberalism, and absence of democracy

There are many common assumptions in mainstream discourse about our globalized world that need to be examined carefully by critical global citizens. "The political and the economic are separate realms;" "Globalization exists apart from politics;" "Capitalism is compatible with democracy while socialism is compatible with dictatorship;" "The free market is a natural phenomenon;" "Neoliberalism is the new liberation of the free market."

These assumptions blend together and become parts of a grand mystification, and it is the difficult task of critical global citizens to demystify it. The case of Cuba-US relations can serve this task, and that is my aim. I focus on Cuba's National Literacy Campaign as a mass movement of critical global citizenship that must be viewed within the context of its historical roots and its legacy. One cannot understand the Campaign without understanding the broader Cuban Revolution, and vice versa. The Revolution followed a long pattern of historical struggles for freedom. Today the Revolution continues to struggle as the global order of neoliberalism punishes Cuba for its disobedience.

Neoliberalism is a term that expresses the full force of globalized capitalism today. Economic liberalism was a global movement in the middle of the 19th Century to transfer economic and political power from monarchs and churches to the noble class of educated landowners. Neoliberalism is the current global economic movement with three objectives (Stromquist, 2002). First, it seeks to diminish or eliminate government regulations on markets, such as tariffs, environmental standards, worker safety laws, minimum wage, and taxes on corporate profits. Second, it has a goal to privatize many services that traditionally have been provided by the public sector. Third, it pressures governments to minimize spending on social services such as education, health care, and social security.

There is nothing natural about these aims of neoliberalism. They are policies made by global elites for the benefit of global elites. A global network supports neoliberalism systematically and undemocratically. The World Bank and International Monetary Fund (IMF) often provide loans to developing nations upon conditions that they adhere to the objectives of neoliberalism. The World Trade Organization (WTO) administers rules of global trade, also with a bias in favor of neoliberalism. There is no democratic accountability over these organizations. They serve the interests of global capital with power to bully governments into compliance. The WTO claims to make decisions by consensus among representatives of member nations, but transnational corporations use carrots and sticks to guide who can become the representatives and how they will vote. An example of this is how the WTO claims to protect intellectual property rights as it prohibits townships in South Africa from receiving free AIDS drugs (Klein, 2007).

Cuba, although it withdrew its memberships with the World Bank and IMF shortly after the Revolution triumphed, joined the WTO in 1995 as a way to garner international support for ending the blockade. The WTO has overseen grievances from Cuban immigrants in the US regarding private enterprises and industries that Cuba nationalized. The most notable recent case has been that of Bacardi Rum, formerly from Cuba and now in Puerto Rico, challenging Cuba in its right to use the label Havana Club Rum, which Bacardi had acquired before 1959 and Cuba nationalized in 1960.

The Cuban Revolution has been determined to set its own course politically and economically. As the Cuban government began in 1959 to nationalize industries formerly owned and operated by private national and international corporations, it offered to compensate these corporations, which mostly were from the US, through twenty-year bonds with 4.5 percent annual interest up to the amount of assets the corporations had claimed to own when assessed for taxation in Cuba (Farber, 2006). The US government rejected the offer and demanded full payments for higher totals. Cuba had begun payments but stopped after diplomatic relations ended between the two countries. Cuba turned to the Soviet Union for oil supplies in 1960 when US refineries refused to deliver oil, and that was the beginning of a long-term trade partnership in which the Soviet Union gave Cuba favorable terms.

Over the decades since 1959, Cuba has implemented several policy changes regarding nationalization or moderate deregulation of small businesses and industries. The collapse of the Soviet Union brought the end of Cuba's advantageous trade relations, and Cuba entered difficult economic times in the early 1990s known as the Special Period. The US government tried to deal the Cuban Revolution a death blow through the Torricelli and Helms-Burton Acts, which increased economic sanctions for international companies trading with Cuba. In response, Cuba allowed an increase in foreign investment while turning to tourism as a vehicle for economic recovery. Terrorist attacks on hotels aimed to undermine tourism resulted in the death of an Italian vacationer in 1997, but Cuba's economy continued to grow gradually.

Today, the global beneficiaries of neoliberalism continue to speculate on the prospects of doing business in Cuba their way. They perpetuate the idea through the media that the end of Fidel Castro's leadership marks the possible beginning of a substantial change in the nation's political economy. In this way they depend on the myth that Cuba has been a totalitarian state. In reality, Cuba's government operates democratically to different degrees at municipal, provincial, and national levels without the corrupting influence of privately financed campaigns. The citizens of Cuba directly nominate and elect their representatives in the municipal assemblies of *Poder Popular*, or People's Power, and they vote to confirm or to reject single candidates at the provincial and national levels. Fidel Castro, as a delegate of the national assembly, was accountable to the vote of his constituents, but they never voted him out of office. Castro continued to lead the country as military commander after his early successes with the Revolutionary War and the defense against the Playa Girón invasion.

What threatens neoliberalism most are its exposure as being fundamentally anti-democratic and the growth of democratic socialism in developing countries. The image of the Castro brothers as dictators, which ignores the extent to which Cubans participate in democratic elections for the legislative branch, certainly has given the right wing in the US its strategy for discrediting the Cuban Revolution. What is especially troublesome now to global capitalism, though, is the emergence of democratically elected governments in South America that openly are rejecting neoliberalism. The Bush Administration failed to enact the pro-business Free Trade Agreement of the Americas because of grassroots opposition in many Latin American countries. The strongest positions against Washington's version of free trade have come from Venezuela, Bolivia and Ecuador. These three bold governments are moving toward a democratic and humanist socialism on their own terms as they break apart the myth that capitalism is democratic while socialism is totalitarian.

As Cuba continues to keep its socialist project alive despite the ongoing blockade, critical global citizens need to recognize the vast gap that Cuba was first to bridge and how much it has cost. Medical students at the University of Michigan have organized a campaign of relief efforts against the damaging effects of the blockade on the health of Cubans (Medical Students for Cuba, 2006). Each year since 1969, a group of US citizens called the Venceremos Brigade delivers medicines, school supplies, and other goods to Cuba to alleviate shortages. Each person in the Brigade risks a fine of thousands of dollars if prosecuted by the US government for violating the travel ban to Cuba. These displays of solidarity and others have allowed Cubans to separate US citizens from US foreign policy when defining the culprit. After Hurricane Katrina caused its devastation in 2005, the Cuban government immediately offered aid to the victims. The US government refused to accept it, showing its stubborn pride.

Critical global citizenship needs a vocabulary and a concept map for political economy, and one of the most important case studies is in the history and current events of Cuba-US relations. As neoliberalism demonstrates, the economy is political. Cuba took a revolutionary turn away from the rest of Latin America by defying US hegemony. Now other nations in Latin America are following with ballots rather than bullets. Cuba's sacrifices on battlefields and through struggles against the blockade have made it possible for other nations to imagine possibilities for another paradigm. Many

Cubans who were too young to fight in the Revolutionary War
went on to do the hard work of the National Literacy Campaign.
Cuba built its new political and economic identity with the strength
that comes from valuing education as a human right for all. The
success of the Campaign continues to inspire contemporary literacy
campaigns in other nations.

Critical global citizenship, nationalism, and internationalism

Frantz Fanon (1963), while focusing on the global effects of
Eurocentric racism, asserted that colonized people must triumph in
nationalist revolutions followed by proletarian revolutions in order
to have a meaningful freedom. The Cuban Revolution was nationalist and did not become socialist by name until the day after the
US bombed Cuban airports in April of 1961. Cuban nationalism
against colonialism had had a long history. Cubans recognize
Hatuey, the Taíno rebel who fought against the earliest Spanish
invasions, as their first revolutionary leader. After the Spanish had
massacred nearly all of the Taíno and gained control of Cuba, it
was not until the early 19th Century that Cuban nationalism took
hold with the leadership of Félix Varela, a Catholic priest who
showed great courage in opposing slavery and colonialism. Cuba
fought two revolutionary wars in the later half of the century to defeat Spanish imperialism, only to face a more indirect but no less
oppressive imperialism from the US. Cubans experienced a nationalist reawakening in the 1920s, when dissidents led by student
groups resisted the US-supported Machado dictatorship until its
collapse in 1933. This revolt did not result in a lasting independence from colonialism, but it set the stage for a radicalized nationalism and the Revolution two decades later.

Nationalism, whether in regard to ethnicity or political state-
hood, is a source that gives people a sense of belonging. Native
Americans in Canada identify themselves as members of First Nations, and many people of French heritage in Quebec have formed
a nationalist movement with the goal of secession. The Civil Rights
Movement eliminated *de jure* segregation in the US, but it also
spawned nationalist organizations such as the Black Panthers, the

American Indian Movement, and the Brown Berets. These nationalist organizations faced severe governmental repression and never
grew into mass movements; however, their struggles led to the possibilities for institutions of higher education to offer courses and
even degree programs in African American Studies, Native American Studies, and Chicano or Mexican American Studies.

Nationalism is important to citizens of the US, but not in a
monolithic way. Many find a false sense of security in a chauvinistic
nationalism. They learn in school not to question the myth of benevolence of the US toward other nations. To question their government's motives behind a war, they learn, is to be unpatriotic.
They come to see the racism of slavery, Jim Crow, and the forced
removal of Native Americans from their homelands as historical
phases without any legacy in today's 'colorblind' society. This kind
of nationalism, akin to what Michael Parenti (2004) calls superpatriotism, provides a sense of superiority when other aspects of life
leave one feeling powerless. When people become alienated with
unfulfilling work, consumerism, and competitive relationships under the ethos of rugged individualism, they can turn their insecurity
into the idea that they are a part of the most superior and most
powerful country in the world. Others in the US—and I include
myself—identify with a different nationalism, finding hope in struggles throughout US history for social justice from the abolitionist
movement to movements for gender equality to current demands
for affordable housing in post-Katrina New Orleans. We pay attention to mainstream media, but we also learn about our country and
the world through media that are neither owned nor sponsored by
corporations. Our heroes are ordinary people who love justice and
care about people from all nations and nationalities.

Nationalism in Cuba is fundamentally different from the ideas
of nationalism in the US. Cuba continues to assert its national identity after having lived in the shadows of Spain and the US. The
Revolution for a majority of Cubans is the advanced expression of
national liberation. A large minority of Cubans has opposed the
Revolution, though, and many have voted with their feet to live in
Miami and other parts of the US. For all Cubans nationalism is
closely tied to internationalism in relation to the US. The mighty

neighbor to the north has the image of either the hand that feeds or
the grip that strangles. In either case, Cubans cannot ignore the
giant only 90 miles away.

Cuba's internationalism since the triumph of the Revolution
has not been fixated on the US, though. By necessity, Cuba turned
to the Soviet Union for trade after the US imposed its blockade.
This new economic dependence did not, however, translate to political and social dependence. Cuban troops supported anti-colonial
and anti-apartheid military struggles in Africa during the 1960s and
'70s despite a strong disapproval from the Soviet government (Gleijeses, 2002). Although Soviet influence on Cuban education and
culture increased during the '70s, it never approached the magni-
tude of domination. When the Soviet Union collapsed, Cuba faced
severe economic hardship and turned to partnerships with foreign
capital for a growing tourism industry. The US government tightened its economic blockade on Cuba during the '90s, but that did
not stop all foreign companies from doing business with Cuba.
Even during the Special Period of economic recovery, Cuba continued to send educators and doctors to developing countries with
the greatest needs. When US citizens wonder out loud when Cuba
will "open up," they obviously are unaware that Cuba has been
open for international trade and relations – only not on terms that
satisfy self-serving US interests.

Internationalism in the US is complicated. There are those who
not so jokingly suggest that everyone in the world should be able to
vote in US national elections because this single nation holds such
great power over the entire world. The US dominates the world in
terms of wealth, albeit in the hands of fewer and fewer elites, and
military might. Eisenhower warned about the possibility of a military-industrial complex becoming a power unto itself, and now the
US government is still involved in the so-called War on Terror after
neoconservatives attempted to lay a foundation for endless war.
The government, with ample support from Democrats, sold the war
in Iraq to the citizens first with unsubstantiated claims that Iraq
possessed weapons of mass destruction, followed by ludicrous
claims that Saddam Hussein was allied to Al Qaeda. Later we were
told that the mission is to bring democracy to Iraq, which would

result in more democracies in the Middle East and a safer and more secure world. Meanwhile, transnational corporations based in the US and the UK conveniently take control of formerly nationalized Iraqi oil.

Critical global citizenship in the US is a great challenge. The First Amendment provides the freedom to criticize our government, but to do so during this time of war is to be labeled "unpatriotic" or a part of the "blame America first" subgroup. Voters opposed to the war in Iraq put Democratic majorities in both houses of Congress in 2006, but the vast majority of Democrats continued to vote for ongoing funding of the war. In 2008 voters faced the choices of either a transfer of troops from Iraq to Afghanistan under Obama or a military occupation in both countries of possibly 100 years under McCain's vision. Neither major party questioned the wisdom of US perpetuation of the military-industrial complex. The corporate media ignores and marginalizes any candidate who would do so. They excluded Dennis Kucinich from some of the debates during the primary elections for Democrats, claiming that he was too low in polls to be a serious contender. That becomes a self-fulfilling prophecy, though, when the same media willfully ignore dissenting candidates from the beginnings of their campaigns.

Although Obama won the presidency in 2008, critical global citizens of the US will continue to face the challenges of bipartisan support for neoliberalism, the military-industrial complex, the building of a wall along the Mexican border, the less-than-urgent response to global climate change, the push to privatize struggling schools in impoverished districts, and more. Although the US has five percent of the world's population, it consumes about 25 percent of the world's energy resources. The growth that capitalism needs to satisfy wealthy investors is unsustainable. The global policy of neoliberalism is profoundly undemocratic. The fact that nearly a billion people go to bed hungry every night in this world of plenty is a travesty. A world of peace will never be possible when so many people cannot feed their families.

The way US citizens view their place in the world is steeped in a tradition of tunnel vision. The US and Europe tend to divide the world into so-called Western and non-Western civilizations. Applying a negative label puts the "non-Western" societies in a category of the "other." This dehumanizing categorization makes it easier for many "Westerners" to demonize Islam, especially after September 11, 2001. Christine Sleeter (2004) analyzed the state standards for social studies in California for elementary and secondary schools and found that there was us-versus-them language throughout the document along the line of "Western" and "non-Western" societies. School children learn early that "Western" is the standard of civilization by which the rest of the world is measured, and Sleeter poignantly calls this "standardizing imperialism."

Another way of viewing the world is to see the global North and global South. This perspective places the political economy of colonialism and imperialism at the center. Western European empires covered the Americas, Africa and parts of Asia. The US, within 50 years of gaining independence, declared with the Monroe Doctrine that Latin America was off limits to further European colonization. With the exceptions of Puerto Rico, the Virgin Islands, Guantánamo Bay in Cuba, and the canal zone of Panamá, the US did not go on to expropriate lands in Latin America. What happened on a much larger scale was the neocolonialism of US-based transnational corporations exploiting natural resources and human labor throughout the region. The prime example was the United Fruit Company, but many other US industries have jumped at the chance to maximize profits globally. Latin America was part of Europe's global South, and it became the object of the United States' southward Manifest Destiny.

Times are changing, though, in much of Latin America. Cuba was the first to sustain a revolution against neocolonialism. Chile followed with the democratic election of socialist President Salvador Allende in 1970, only to be crushed by a CIA-supported coup d'état that happened on the *other* September 11, in 1973. During the 1980s, the US government covertly funded the *Contra* paramilitary forces to destroy the leftist Sandinista government of Nicaragua. As civil wars escalated in Guatemala and El Salvador, the US supported the armies of right-wing dictators to ensure that no more leftist movements would gain control. The Cold War passed, and the US became the world's sole superpower. John Williamson, a

US economist, coined the term "Washington Consensus" in 1990 in regard to a set of neoliberal policies toward Latin America with the cooperation of the World Bank, the IMF and the US government. Several national governments in Latin America have rejected these policies to varying degrees with the strongest resistance currently coming from Venezuela, Bolivia and Ecuador.

As Latin American nations continue to declare independence from neoliberalism, critical global citizens of the US will have an important role of solidarity. The US government placed Cuba on its list of "state sponsors of terrorism" in 1982, and Cuba remains on that list as of this writing with only three others—Iran, Syria, and Sudan. On April 30, 2007, US Secretary of State Condoleezza Rice classified Venezuela as "not fully cooperating" with US counter-terrorism efforts. Critical global citizens of the US need to investigate through international and independent media how Cuba and Venezuela have received and retained these designations. It will also be necessary to realize how such designations in Latin America might continue in the future with respect to questionable evidence and hidden motives. The US government has a recent track record of using deception to justify the initiation of full-scale wars against Vietnam and Iraq, and the possibility exists for the same in targeting any part of Latin America. When military forces of US-ally Colombia entered Ecuador to kill a rebel leader of the *Fuerzas Armadas Revolucionarias de Colombia* (FARC) on March 3, 2008, both Venezuela and Ecuador immediately expelled Colombian diplomats. Tensions did not escalate, but the event was a spark with the potential for igniting a wildfire.

If not for the wars in Iraq and Afghanistan, the US military might very well be in Venezuela to prevent the Chávez administration from keeping more oil wealth for the people of Venezuela. Just as the US military serves the so-called US interests behind the global giant of neoliberalism, there is a need for a global civil society to resist that power and to create new possibilities for peace with social and economic justice. The concept of critical global citizenship needs to grow in the US to the point where a new paradigm arises beyond the sterile notion that democracy is merely voting for one of the two parties representing Wall Street. Cuba had a revolution before its education became revolutionary. The US is not on the brink of a revolution, but a small and growing cadre of progressive and radical educators can make a big difference. The assumption that schools merely reflect the broader society in which they exist is debilitating and cynical. Educators in the US can foster critical thinking and critical global citizenship in an organized and systematic fashion, and the world eagerly awaits this. Young people, as they did in Cuba's National Literacy Campaign, can collectively become a force for change in the US, and the world eagerly awaits this.

Scope of this book

Cuba's National Literacy Campaign of 1961 set the stage for a new critical global citizenship in Cuba, and the implications were immense for the rest of Latin America and the entire so-called Third World. Cuba's Year of Education, 1961, is the focus of the fourth and fifth of six chapters. Since the meaning of the Campaign can be understood only in context of its antecedent history and its legacy, the remaining four chapters provide a chronological development of articulations between literacy and national identity in Cuba. The concept of critical global citizenship gives a framework throughout the chapters.

The second chapter provides a history of Cuba's pre-Columbian, colonial and neocolonial eras. The focus is on literacy as a key to anti-imperialism and critical global citizenship. I start with the indigenous Taíno culture before and after Spanish conquest. Cuba's first revolutionary leader, Hatuey, led a resistance against the invaders, and he is an important figure in Cuba's multicultural history of struggles for freedom. What follows is Cuba's colonial existence in the Spanish empire and the evolution from organizations for greater autonomy to mobilizations for revolutionary wars. This section highlights movements that joined in efforts to abolish slavery and to demand Cuba's independence. It culminates in the impact of José Martí, the exiled anti-imperialist philosopher, poet and essayist who inspired many Cubans to fight the second revolutionary war against Spain and who remains Cuba's foremost

national hero today. The chapter then addresses the era that followed in the years 1898 to 1958. While focusing on trends in literacy drives, it follows the developments from reformist nationalism
to revolutionary insurrection and war in response to dictatorships
supported by the US. Throughout this second chapter is an expla-
nation of how internationalism, or critical global citizenship, played
important roles in Cuba's reformist and revolutionary movements.

The third chapter looks at critical global citizenship as a source
of strength for Cuba's work after the triumph of the Revolution in
1959, focusing on the work of two years that went into preparations
for the National Literacy Campaign. Literacy became the most urgent priority after land redistribution. Cuba was embracing a process of transforming education from a privilege to a human right.
Armando Hart, Cuba's new Minister of Education, and the newly
formed National Commission for Literacy shared in the leadership
for planning the Campaign. The Commission published a manual
and a primer for instruction in the upcoming Campaign, and these
books contained many themes of nationalism and internationalism
within the goals of the Revolution. This chapter explains how
Cuba's new revolutionary internationalism was an example of critical global citizenship.

The fourth chapter, from a perspective of critical global citizenship, gives a detailed account of 1961 as the Campaign took center
stage in the Year of Education. The government recruited and
trained mainly urban youth, whose average age was 15 to 16, as
instructors for remote rural regions that had been without schools.
Parents gave their documented permission even after the murder of
the young teacher, Conrado Benítez, by counter-revolutionary terrorists during the pilot phase. The US attacks on Cuban airports,
Castro's declaration of the socialist nature of the Revolution, and
the Bay of Pigs invasion all occurred in April as the mass mobilization of the Campaign was underway. Cuba's successful defense
against the invasion brought new energy to the Campaign. As rural
families became literate, the young instructors learned from them
about the hard work of living off of the land. Landless peasants had
been the majority of fighters in the Revolutionary War against Batista's army, and then relatively privileged urban youth were ex-

changing the gift of reading and writing for the perspective of those who had been at the center of the military struggles for a national transformation. The government urged all who could teach to do so and all who needed to learn to do so. Literate workers taught illiterate co-workers, and urban dwellers taught neighbors. The rural families that became literate were working through the lessons and toward the final assignment of writing a letter to Castro. The November murder of another instructor, Manuel Ascunce, brought grief but also greater resolve to finish the work. One by one, municipalities across Cuba declared themselves to be free of illiteracy. The national celebration at the end of the Campaign occurred in Havana on December 22, and the young instructors were home for Christmas. This chapter, as well, presents ongoing themes of internationalism in light of critical global citizenship.

The fifth chapter is where I present and comment on excerpts of testimonies from Cubans who participated in the Campaign. These testimonies are from about 100 people who in 2003 shared with me their experiences in 1961 and their thoughts in interviews and focus groups. Although I captured their words on transcripts, I often am reminded of how much the printed words do not reveal the passion behind the spoken expressions. As a doctoral student, I did not have the resources to video-tape the communications. I have tried my best in this chapter to represent the spirit behind the participants' words, knowing that it is impossible to capture it fully. I had some difficulty limiting the number of testimonies to include, and I chose to allow several themes to appear while emphasizing critical global citizenship.

The sixth and final chapter considers the national and international legacies of the Campaign. Cuba's newly literate, numbering about 707,000, continued to learn in a follow-up program called Battle for the Sixth Grade. Schools appeared for the first time in many rural zones. The government enforced compulsory education for all children through the ninth grade and provided free tuition through graduate school. This national transformation of education has made Cuba a leader in literacy rates among Latin American nations. As other nations around the world have needed assistance for literacy drives or medical care, Cuba has sent many professionals. Cuban youth grow up learning a critical global citizenship of solidarity with all nations that likewise have suffered underdevelopment through colonialism and neocolonialism. As such nations stand up for their rights to have genuine sovereignty and alternatives to the neoliberal status quo, they can understand the struggles and possibilities through Cuba's experience with critical global citizenship.

Several writings on Cuba's National Literacy Campaign already exist in English, and my hope is that this book provides a new perspective with regard to critical global citizenship. The Campaign was a great success for the Cuban Revolution, and it merits much greater attention than it has received in English print. This book places the Campaign in contexts of history and legacy while highlighting the importance of critical global citizenship throughout Cuba's struggles for national sovereignty. As of this writing, President Barack Obama has kept his promise to continue the damaging economic blockade on Cuba. Global condemnations of the blockade through UN votes have not been enough to persuade US leaders to end the aggression. It will end only if more US citizens take time to learn the history of US-Cuba relations and then apply pressure on their representatives in Washington for change. Schools, churches, unions, and many more potential sites of education and action need to explore how Cuba can be a source of hope for all nations struggling for meaningful sovereignty. It takes time and commitment to gain an understanding of neoliberalism today and its predecessor that is colonialism. This account of Cuba's National Literacy Campaign can be one piece of a grand puzzle that can expose the current oppressive and undemocratic realities of globalization in its current state. It might be true that globalization is inevitable, but it can be made more democratic, more just, and more sustainable with the help of more attention toward critical global citizenship.

2. Literacy and Citizenship for Resistance in a Colonized Land

The term 'global citizenship' was not coined until late in the 20th century, but Cubans have lived in a forced global reality through the ages that has shaped them into citizens of the world. As a nation they have endured colonialism and neocolonialism from Spain and the US, respectively, and the latter still exerts tremendous pressure. Cuba's global position is more than its defense against outside domination, though. It is also the identification with all of Latin America and with all of the so-called Third World. Cuba is a pioneer nation in its struggle for sovereignty in a world where neoliberalism has taken the place of nation-building empires. In order to understand the critical global citizenship of Cubans today, one needs to study its colonial and neocolonial past in light of literacy, nationalism, and internationalism.

Cuba is a land with a turbulent history. First, the indigenous Taíno nation of the Greater Antilles faced attacks from the Carib nation of the Lesser Antilles. Then Columbus and the Spaniards arrived, enslaving the Taíno and decimating them with massacres and new diseases. Spain ruled Cuba along with Puerto Rico and the Philippines until 1898. A growing nationalism and anti-slavery movement in Cuba throughout the 19th Century culminated in two wars for independence. As José Martí (1999) predicted, the US replaced Spain as an imperialist obstacle to sovereignty. The rebellion against Machado's US-supported dictatorship in the late 1920s met with violent reaction, but a mass uprising expelled the regime in 1933. What might have been a new beginning for Cuba was destroyed when Batista took *de facto* power through a coup d'état. Batista's second dictatorship in the 1950s, though, met with an insurrection that grew into an overwhelming revolution. All of these phases of struggle have become parts of Cuba's national and international identities. An understanding of the Cuban Revolution and its Literacy Campaign requires a careful study of Cuba's long history of struggles against colonialism, slavery, and illiteracy. Embedded in these struggles are themes of internationalism as well as nationalism.

Cuba's first revolutionary: Hatuey

All nations have heroes. Cuba has its share, and the earliest one that Cubans celebrate is Hatuey, the Taíno warrior who led a resistance against Spanish invaders. Having witnessed a massacre of Taíno people in Hispaniola, he fled with others to warn the Taíno in what is now Cuba of the threat that the Spanish posed, showing them gold and telling them how the Spanish worshipped it as a god. Hatuey led a resistance against the Spanish who arrived in Baracoa in 1510 until they captured him and other resisters in 1512 and burned them at the stake.

Hatuey's legend lives on in the stories told by Taíno still in Cuba and in the writings of Barolomé de las Casas, the Dominican friar who arrived in the Caribbean in 1502 and chronicled and protested against slavery and other cruelties of the Spanish toward the Taíno. Cubans widely recognize Hatuey as their first revolutionary. It is interesting that the US finds its most recognizable indigenous hero in Pocahontas, who aided the European conquest of North America, while Cuba celebrates Hatuey and the resistance he represents (Chomsky, Carr & Smorkaloff, 2003). This kind of distinction is important in light of critical global citizenship, which recognizes indigenous rights as human rights and affirms indigenous knowledge as a key to understanding our humanity, diversity, and possibilities. Hatuey's resistance more than 500 years ago is connected to the current resistance of the indigenous Zapatistas in Chiapas, México. The Zapatistas' brief armed rebellion on New Year's Day of 1994 gave way to a non-violent but determined struggle to regain land rights lost in the North American Free Trade Agreement (NAFTA), and a worldwide network has responded with devoted solidarity to the first revolutionary movement to be posted on the Internet.

The Colony's Early Educational Reformism

In the second decade of the 19th Century, Simón Bolívar led the rebellion in the northern part of South America that sparked a fire throughout Latin America. While Spain was fighting to regain its independence from Napoleon, its American colonies began their own fights for independence. Many of these colonies gained independence in the early 1820s, but Cuba and Puerto Rico remained under the Spanish crown until 1898. Cuba's steps toward national autonomy began with reformist educational movements and grew with a crescendo to two revolutionary wars. Also growing were the themes of abolishing slavery and illiteracy.

Spain knew in the 18th Century that it was falling behind other European nations in the quest for economic power. As a result, a royal decree established the Royal Economic Society of Friends of the Nation in 1775. Local chapters of this organization appeared throughout Spain and some of its colonies. Founded in 1793, the Cuban chapter, like other local and regional chapters, took the organization's name without the "Royal." Cuba's *Sociedad Económica de Amigos del País* [Economic Society of Friends of the Nation] (SEAP), influenced by the American and French Revolutions, developed a reformist agenda for *criollo* interests in the colony. *Criollos*, Cubans born of entirely Spanish ancestry, were second in power only to the Spanish-born aristocracy in Cuba. Native American or African ancestry resulted in less power in the racialized colonial societies, and Spain replaced Native Americans with Africans for slavery after European diseases decimated indigenous populations.

Cuba's SEAP focused on developments in arts and sciences, and in 1816 it created an Education Section, which reported on the state of education in Cuba while studying educational advances around the world (Pérez Cruz, 2001). Reports included the creation of schools and scholarships for poor children. By 1836, the section started planning to create Cuba's first school for adult literacy. SEAP gradually advanced the idea of Cuban nationalism, but it never declared an opposition to slavery.

SEAP presented a cautious reformism to advance Cuban society through education, but there were other voices that pushed matters more urgently. José Augustín Caballero wrote the Ordinances of the Free Schools of Havana in 1794, insisting on education for mathematics and language and calling for a plan to combat illiteracy. A census in 1774 placed Cuba's illiteracy rate at 60 percent (Pérez Cruz, 2001), a figure that most likely did not account for slaves. This first outcry for eliminating illiteracy would grow along with the development of a more radical nationalism in Cuba.

Idea of independence takes hold

Free Cubans of African descent learned about the Haitian Revolution of 1791 to 1804, and they became leaders of the first organized rebellions with Cuban independence and the abolition of slavery as goals. Nicolás Morales, a free black Cuban, formed such a group as early as 1795, but he was betrayed by a mulatto man who received a reward of 200 acres of land (Gott, 2004). A larger rebellion emerged in 1810, taking advantage of Spain's preoccupation in fighting against Napoleon. This uprising called for Cuban independence but not for an end to slavery. Led by white Cubans but with a significant black militia, it ignited racist fear in Havana's white population, which formed its own militia. The rebellion was crushed in the same year. Another planned rebellion, led by a free black Cuban named José Antonio Aponte in 1812, was unequivocally determined to achieve Cuban independence and the abolition of slavery. A betrayal alerted the colonial authorities, though, and they captured and beheaded Aponte.

Black Cubans (hereafter "Afro-Cubans," as commonly used in Cuba) catalyzed the independence movement with the hope of ending slavery. Their cause gained the unlikely support of a member of the white leadership in the Catholic Church. Felix Varela, an influential priest, became the best known figure in the first half of the 19th Century for advancing the agenda for Cuban independence. In addition to his support for Latin American independence, he took the unpopular position for the abolition of slavery. When a Cuban section of Bolívar's movement called 'Soles y Rayos de Bolívar' emerged in the early 1820s, the government reaction forced Varela into exile, first to Spain and later to the US. From the US, until his death in 1853, he wrote journal articles for Cuban intellectuals in hopes that the cause for independence would accelerate. Today Varela's name is invoked by Cubans in projects across the political spectrum.

José Antonio Saco, a journal editor and disciple of Varela, became the first Cuban to design a mass literacy campaign (Pérez Cruz, 2001; Gott, 2004). He was much less enlightened than Varela, though. His criticism of colonial rule fell short of a call for independence, and he became associated with a racist movement for a white Cuba. Saco wrote in 1937 that he always wanted autonomy for Cubans but felt it could never happen. He argued that Cuba's best hope would involve an association with the US, and this position grew among many Cuban and US citizens. Indeed, the US government had declared in the Monroe Doctrine of 1823 that Latin America would no longer be a new imperial domain for European nations, implying that the US had sole power to colonize its neighbors to the South.

Another disciple of Varela was José de la Luz y Caballero, a philosopher who became an important influence on José Martí. Luz y Caballero was the first Cuban to speak of education as a science. He saw education as much more than instruction, as the source for "moderating the soul for life" (Luz y Cabellero, quoted in Pérez Cruz, 2001, p. 14). Although he was not explicitly calling for an independence movement, his advocacy for active student learning and critical thinking helped to set the stage for a more revolutionary nationalism in Cuba. Education of the kind that Luz y Caballero promoted became a source of worry for the colonial government, which issued the *Plan de Estudios* [Plan of Studies] in 1844. This policy had three objectives: 1) to centralize and control education in the hands of the colonial governor, 2) to break up the bases of the Cuban intellectual movement, and 3) to shape the education system into an institution of political hegemony under loyalty to the Spanish Crown. The Catholic Church also served the interests of colonialism, but Father Varela had been an exception.

England abolished slavery at home and in the West Indies in 1833 and urged Spain to follow suit, but Spain continued to rely on Cuban slavery for maximizing profits in the sugar industry. A massive Cuban slave revolt of 1843 and 1844 known as *La Escalera* [the staircase] ended with a severe repression, including indiscriminate lynching, against Afro-Cubans. More white Cubans began to view the US as their only hope to alleviate their racist fears. During the 1850s, two US presidents, Franklin Pierce and James Buchanan, attempted to annex Cuba. Pierce, an anti-abolitionist looking to expand US slavery, tried to purchase Cuba from Spain, but Spain refused. The Ostend Manifesto, containing the offer to Spain and written by Pierce's ministers to Spain, France, and England, warned against allowing "Cuba to be Africanized and become a second St. Domingo [referring to Haiti], with all its attendant horrors to the white race" (quoted in Franklin, 1997, p. 5). Buchanan, Pierce's successor, tried to persuade Congress into buying Cuba, but Congress was too divided over slavery.

It was not until the 1860s that an educational movement would bring Cuban nationalism out of hiding. José Silverio Jorrín, as President of SEAP in 1865, proposed that traveling teachers educate children of willing parents in rural zones that had no schools (Pérez Cruz, 2001). He began to organize Cuba's first mass literacy campaign, but it never came to fruition. Jorrín fled Cuba in 1869 to save himself from the colonialist terror in Cuba's First War of Independence, which had started a year earlier. Rafael Morales began literacy and academic courses for adult workers in 1866 with the goals of Cuban independence and abolition of slavery. His work became illegal, but he refused to stop.

From Varela to Luz y Caballero to Morales, there was a current of critical global citizenship that demanded dignity for Cuba and Cubans. When peaceful means for claiming human rights were thwarted, war became a matter of honor and self defense. As Cubans took up arms in 1868 to end slavery and colonialism, they continued to advance their fight against illiteracy and ignorance. They became revolutionary in their determination to destroy the chains of oppression and to create a new and promising homeland for Cubans.

Cuba's First War of Independence

Cuba's First War of Independence, also called the Ten Years War, started on October 10, 1868. On that day plantation owner Carlos Manuel de Céspedes, in the company of friends and slaves, shouted the *Grito of Yara* [*grito* being the "yell" that other Spanish colonies had made to declare independence]. Céspedes then freed and armed his slaves. The rebellion spread quickly with free Afro-Cubans and liberated slaves joining the ranks. Máximo Gómez, the Dominican general who had led other independence wars, joined the rebels as did many Dominican fighters. *Mambí* had been a derogatory name in Santo Domingo aimed at people of African descent, but the Cuban rebels adopted it as a source of pride (Gott, 2004).

The Manifesto of Carlos Manuel de Céspedes included a condemnation of colonial education. It chastised Spain for wanting the Cuban people to be ignorant and unable to recognize their rights as humans. Many teachers joined the *Mambí* forces despite threats by the colonial army that they would be shot if captured. Morales promoted free and universal education in liberated regions with the Law of Public Instruction, the first of its kind in Cuba. This law developed a popular education that included the history and geography of Cuba. Morales also distributed a letter to all liberated zones demanding that illiteracy be eradicated. *Mambí* pedagogy became an example of revolutionary popular education that Cubans would remember in future struggles for national emancipation (Pérez Cruz, 2001).

The war took on all the elements of race that had divided Cubans. Many white Cubans joined the colonial army out of fear of the strong Afro-Cuban representation in the *Mambí* forces. Antonio Maceo, an Afro-Cuban who had been free before the war, became a *Mambí* leader of the Afro-Cuban rebels and a great military strategist. His strategy, which gained the blessing of Céspedes, was to organize a slave rebellion and to bring more liberated slaves into the *Mambí* ranks. The rebels destroyed many plantations, and their numbers grew as they welcomed the freed slaves.

Both sides struggled on through the years without the ability to
end with a convincing victory. The Pact of Zanjón of 1878 brought
an unsettled peace. Neither independence nor the abolition of slavery triumphed, but the colonial authorities agreed to some conces-
sions. Slaves who had fought for the *Mambí* were freed, along with
Chinese indentured workers. The government prohibited racial
discrimination in businesses open to the public and ordered public
schools to admit all children regardless of color. Maceo expressed
his unwillingness to accept anything short of independence and
abolition when he met shortly after Zanjón with Arsenio Martínez
Campos, the leader of Cuba's military. A few rebellions raged on
during the Guerra Chiquita [Little War] of 1879 and 1880, but a
white leader of the rebels, Calixto García, prevented Maceo from
leading what might be perceived as a race war. Many grew tired of
fighting, and a harsh repression against Afro-Cubans followed the
surrender. Slavery finally ended in 1886, and the struggle for independence found renewed energy with the leadership of José Martí.

Martí and revolutionary education

José Martí remains Cuba's most celebrated national hero, and
all of Latin America honors his contributions to independence. As
an essayist, poet, teacher, and philosopher, he wrote many volumes
on a variety of subjects. Although not a Marxist, he was a revolutionary advocate for ending imperialism and slavery. Like Varela,
Martí was banished from the remaining Spanish empire.

Born to Spanish immigrants in Havana in 1853, Martí, like his
parents, was a product of the colonial government's plan to 'whiten'
the population. At age 12 he entered a school directed by the poet
Rafael María de Mendive, who had been influenced by Varela and
Luz y Caballero (Kirk, 1983). Martí was arrested at age 16 for sub-
versive writings honoring the rebels of the war for independence. In
1870 his parents managed to have his six-year sentence of exile on
Isle of Pines changed to a deportation to Spain.

Martí studied philosophy and law at Madrid's Central University and learned from the writings of Julián Sans del Rio, who became an important influence throughout the Spanish-speaking

world in the field of education (Gott, 2004). He became more radicalized in 1871 when eight medical students were executed in Havana for protesting against Spanish imperialism. He traveled and
taught in Mexico and Central America before returning to Cuba in
1878. The next year he was again deported to Spain after being
charged with conspiracy in the Guerra Chiquita. He then moved
clandestinely to New York to work with other Cuban exiles in
planning the next war for independence.

During his years in New York, Martí wrote prolifically and
emerged as Cuba's leading voice for independence. He warned
against an imperialistic United States increasing its control over
Latin America, which he called "Our America." Although critical
of Marxism, he also scorned the capitalism of the US in its violent
repression against organized labor. He wrote in defense of indigenous rights and in favor of the internationalism inspired by Bolívar,
but his main focus remained Cuba's independence. In 1890 he established the *Liga de Instrucción*, an organization for training a cadre
of revolutionary teachers and workers among the mostly black Cubans living in New York. He wrote in 1892 of a need to unite Cubans within one party, the Cuban Revolutionary Party. Then he
abandoned his writing to make plans with Generals Gómez and
Maceo for the Second War of Independence. Martí died in battle in
Cuba as that war was beginning in 1895.

Martí's essays on education have had a profound impact on
Cuban society. He wrote of the roles of education regarding national identity, Latin American internationalism, and liberty. He
promoted compulsory education for all minors, equal educational
opportunities between girls and boys, popular education for adults,
and campaigns to eradicate illiteracy. In 1884 Martí (1990b) fore-
saw the need throughout Latin America to send teachers to rural
zones in order to bring literacy to *campesinos* [peasants] when he
wrote, "The traveling school is the only way to eliminate peasant
ignorance" (p. 52, my translation). All of these ideas and more from
Martí informed the planning and implementation of Cuba's National Literacy Campaign of 1961. His contribution to critical
global citizenship was revolutionary, and Cuba's present revolu-

tionary government cannot be understood without an understanding of Martí.

From Spanish colonialism to US neocolonialism

Upon Martí's death in 1895, Salvador Cisneros Betancourt, a veteran of the First War of Independence, became the provisional president of the insurgency. Cuba's Second War for Independence, much like the First, troubled white racist fears. Winston Churchill wrote in a US magazine that the rebel army is "an undisciplined rabble" that consists "to a large extent of coloured men" and that a rebel triumph would mean "Cuba will be a black republic" (as quoted by Gott, p. 92). Gómez and Maceo led the rebels, armed with machetes for cutting sugar cane, to many victorious battles, and Spain sent General Valeriano Weyler to Cuba in 1896 with a counter-guerrilla strategy. Weyler moved entire towns and villages into what were called 'reconcentration camps', depriving the rebel army of new recruits and support. Many of the camps were lacking food, and an international outcry called for Spain to end the cruel policy. Momentum turned in favor of the Spanish army, and Maceo's death in battle brought further grief to the rebels. The 1897 assassination of Spanish Prime Minister Antonio Cánovas brought new hope that Weyler's camps would be liberated and that Cuba would be independent at last. Weyler resigned due to his unpopularity in the US, but Spain's peace agreement with the Philippines allowed more troops to go to Cuba and continue the war there.

A turning point in the history of the Americas and the world came with the sinking of the US battleship *Maine* on February 15, 1898. This accident in Havana's harbor, in which 258 US sailors died, became an opportunity for the US to blame a Spanish mine and enter the war apparently on the side of Cuba. The yellow journalism of William Randolph Hearst, owner of the *New York Journal*, set the drumbeat for war that became irresistible to the US public. Trumbull White (1898), a popular historian and war correspondent in the US, wrote that the sailors did not die in vain "for it is their death that will be remembered as the culminating influence for American intervention and the salvation of scores of thousands of

lives of starving Cuban women and children" (p. 37). Truly, Cubans did suffer greatly in the war against Spain and lost some
300,000 lives. What remained to be seen was whether Cuba could
become independent from the US after its recovery.

The US declared war on Spain in April of 1898 and sped to
victory. The US called it the Spanish-American War, but Cuba
named it the US intervention in Cuba's War for independence.
Cuba was not represented at the armistice in August. The Treaty of
Paris in December gave the US four new possessions: Cuba, Puerto
Rico, the Philippines and Guam. As the Spanish military left Cuba,
the US forces remained in occupation. Meanwhile, a revolt in the
Philippines in 1899 turned into a war against the new colonizers
from the US. President McKinley claimed that Filipinos attacked
US forces first, but several US troops later spoke of receiving orders
to fire the first shots in order to provoke a battle (Zinn, 2001).

Historian Louis A. Pérez Jr. (2008) reports on how images of
Cubans as helpless children, first appearing in US media early in
the 19th Century, have contributed to an imperialist outlook in the
US toward Cuba. As the US entered the Spanish-American War,
the media exploited images showing racist stereotypes of Cubans,
Puerto Ricans and Filipinos in many cartoons. John J. Johnson
(2003) wrote, "Cubans are not only infantilized; they are frequently
represented as blacks who are alternately cheerful, irresponsible,
lazy, dim, and grotesquely deformed" (p. 135). By contrast, Uncle
Sam is portrayed as the strong fatherly figure bringing civilization
to the new US territories in the name of the so-called white man's
burden.

Amidst the patriotic fever of expansionism, there were US citizens who protested the outcomes of the Spanish American War,
especially as the insurgency in the Philippines continued for years
despite the massacres at the hands of US troops. On this war Mark
Twain commented, "We have pacified some thousands of the is-
landers and buried them; destroyed their fields; burned their villages, and turned their widows and orphans out-of-doors" (quoted
in Zinn, 2001). The Anti-Imperialist League formed in 1898 as a
group of US professionals and intellectuals concerned about US
aggression abroad, and they made efforts to inform the public of

the horrors taking place in the Philippines. They were deeply involved in critical global citizenship in the face of a chauvinist nationalism. Labor unions in the US, though, were split, many favoring the annexation of the Philippines despite the blatant capitalist expansionism. This division of the working class, mirroring the domestic racism common in many unions, ensured that a unified class struggle would not occur anytime soon.

While Cubans did not revolt against US occupation as did the Filipinos, they began to realize that their independence was questionable. The US military occupation, headed by Generals John Brooke and Leonard Wood, extended political and economic privileges to affluent white Cubans who had returned from exile in the US. Many non-Cuban US Citizens followed to seek new opportunities as the war-torn island moved toward recovery. The economy was falling squarely into the hands of those who came from the North.

President McKinley ordered General Wood to prepare Cubans for a republican form of government and to set up a school system. Wood adapted the existing schools to a US orientation, having textbooks translated from English to Spanish and having teachers travel to the US for retraining. Protestant missionaries arrived in Cuba to establish schools and to begin the work of converting Catholics. The Methodists in particular offered a segregated education for the white elite (Gott, 2004).

US intentions of a prolonged hegemony over Cuba became clear with the Platt Amendment of 1901, which was passed by the US Congress, signed by President McKinley, and placed within Cuba's new Constitution. With this document Cuba consented to any future military intervention deemed necessary by the US government in order to preserve Cuba's independence. Although Cuba was not an outright colony of the US, it became a prime example of neocolonialism—experiencing political, economic and social penetration from a more powerful nation while wearing the masquerade of a dubious independence.

Education in the new Cuban republic

Tomás Estrada Palma of the Republican Party was unopposed as he was elected Cuba's first president in 1901, but General Wood's supervision ensured that the election commission would be rigged in Estrada's favor and that Afro-Cubans, women, and all people with less than $250 would not vote. The US military occupation ended in 1902 as Estrada took office, but US economic penetration only grew. US individuals or corporations owned 60% of rural properties as early as 1905 (Franklin, 1997; Gott, 2004). Estrada sought re-election in 1906, and his opponent in the Liberal Party, José Miguel Gómez, withdrew under signs of another rigged election process. An insurrection resulted, and the US Marines returned to Cuba in 1906 to restore order. Estrada then resigned in protest after President Theodore Roosevelt sent Secretary of War William Howard Taft to mediate between Estrada and the Liberals. A US lawyer named Charles Magoon replaced Taft and ruled Cuba with Marines present until 1909, shortly after Gómez was elected President.

Cuba's educational thought in the early 20th Century went in three directions (Pérez Cruz, 2001). One was a clandestine struggle against the Catholic Church and the bourgeoisie, who were allies of US imperialism. This struggle grew and became more open in the 1920s. Another was the reformist bourgeois ideal of modern development but with a Cuban nationalist identity. Enrique José Varona, a Cuban intellectual who had lived in the US, was an important leader in this direction. The third and prevalent direction, emanating from the Spanish clergy, upheld the US model that kept education in control of interests.

Education continued to be a privilege of the elite as it had been in the Spanish colony. The illiteracy rate was at 43.4 percent in 1907 (Pérez Cruz, 2001). Fidel Miro, a former *Mambí* soldier, formed a literacy drive in 1907 called the Federated Workers' National Order of ABCs, but it did not receive enough support to grow beyond its base in Santa Clara. Cuban educators skillfully worked within the functionalist educational program that specialist Alexis Frye brought from the U.S. Since Varona had lived in the

U.S., many Cuban educational leaders were familiar with this program and considered it to be not necessarily negative for Cuba. The second US military occupation, from 1906 to 1909, did nothing to improve education in Cuba, and more educators became disillusioned with the system that brought benefits to a minority of Cubans. Funds for education dropped with the price of sugar. Local and provincial government officials began to demand that schools adopt a more nationalist curriculum that questioned the US influence in Cuba (Quiroz, 2001). Cuban nationalism was a defiant position that emerged from experience first with colonialism and then from neocolonialism. This was an important step toward critical global citizenship making its way into the schools.

Varona led several educators in 1917 to found the Pedagogical Action Program, and it grew into a nationalist, bourgeois movement (Pérez Cruz, 2001). One of its leaders, Ramiro Guerra, proposed several education reforms, including a plan to fight illiteracy. The movement focused on developing the sciences and promoted education as a science. Though influential, it never opposed neocolonialism. When Machado moved Cuba toward a US-supported dictatorship in 1925, Guerra was his willing Minister of Education.

The US occupations of Cuba's first decade as a republic set back much of the progress that the *Mambí* had made toward racial equality. Only a few Afro-Cubans gained positions of prestige and only if they were clearly loyal to the order. More than 10,000 Afro-Cubans joined the Independent Party of Color (PIC) by 1910. Led by Evaristo Estenoz, a former slave and war veteran, the party sought more hiring of Afro-Cubans in public sector jobs. After the party was banned, it became more militant in its struggles for racial justice. Around 4,000 members followed Estenoz in armed rebellion in 1912, and the government responded with a massacre of an estimated 3,000 insurgents. The US military refused to intervene for the protection of Afro-Cubans, but Marines did land at the US base at Guantánamo Bay with orders to protect US sugar plantations in the region (Helg, 1995; Gott, 2004).

Estenoz was among those killed. He wrote the party's program in 1908, calling for an independent and sovereign Cuba without racial divisions (Estenoz, 2003). Specific platform items for change included jury trials, abolition of the death penalty, an eight-hour workday, a Labor Tribunal, and land for war veterans. There were also several items regarding education, including school for youthful offenders, free and compulsory education for ages six to fourteen, free and compulsory vocational schools for adults, free university education, state regulation of private education, and the creation of a Naval and Military Academy. Many of these progressive ideas reappeared with the Cuban Revolution that triumphed in 1959.

Critical global citizenship finds a part of its foundation in critical race theory, making historical connections between indigenous struggles for sovereignty and emancipation of the African Diaspora. Also part of its foundation is international feminism. Cuba's first wave of feminist thought emerged early in the 20th Century. As with its counterpart in the US, women's right to vote was the central demand. In other ways, though, early Cuban feminism set itself apart from the US movement. While US feminists used a discourse of equal rights within individualism, Cuban feminists called for patriotism and complementary, not equal, roles between the sexes (Chomsky, Carr & Smorkaloff, 2003). The National Women's Congress had its first two meetings in Havana in 1923 and 1925. One of the topics of the Second Congress involved the status of so-called illegitimate children, and socialist feminist activist Ofelia Domínguez Navarro argued that they should be granted the same rights as legitimate children.   Another part of the foundation of critical global citizenship is a progressive critique of political economy. The capitalism of the US was the dominant force shaping Cuba's economy from 1898 to 1958. As soon as the war against Spain ended, US corporations and individuals began taking over railroad, mine, sugar, tobacco, and lumber industries. United Fruit bought 1,900,000 acres of land for sugar cultivation at about 20 cents an acre. When Havana workers began a general strike in 1899 to call for an eight-hour work day, US troops arrested 11 strike leaders. This reaction set the pattern for strikes that followed, and hundreds of strikers were arrested (Zinn, 2001).

For Cuban workers it became clear that the military occupation was more about protecting US economic interests than safeguard-

ing Cuba's independence. The tradition of organized labor in Cuba
had started in 1866 with the Association of Tobacco Workers of
Havana. The Socialist Party of Cuba became the young nation's
first Marxist party in 1906. Anarcho-syndicalists formed the Workers Federation of Havana in 1920 (Pérez Cruz, 2001).

The 1920s became a pivotal decade in the growth of a proletarian educational movement in Cuba. Falling sugar prices in 1920
permitted more US investors to buy land at bargain rates, and Cuban landowners became peasants. US troops had returned in 1917
to subdue an uprising of the Liberal Party that claimed fraud in the
1916 presidential election. They remained for training in Cuba
during the First World War and did not leave until 1922. An alliance of university students with urban and rural workers emerged
in opposition to Cuba's capitalist and directions. Leading this new
educational movement was Julio Antonio Mella, recognized by
Cubans today as their first great communist leader.

A common misconception is that Latin American communism
is synonymous with Cuba and Castro, but Mella in the 1920s had
contemporaries in South America. Aníbal Ponce of Argentina
wrote about education from a Marxist perspective. He criticized
bourgeois trends that tried to change education without addressing
class antagonisms. José Mariátegui of Perú wrote about the need for
indigenous peoples, industrial workers, and landless peasants to
form an alliance against the exploitations of the capitalist class. The
Russian Revolution had provided an example of proletarian revolution in Europe, and Latin America began to grow its own roots of
class struggle.

Many of Mella's (1975) writings are published in *J. A. Mella:
Documentos y Artículos* [Documents and articles]. Mella became radicalized in 1923 in the Congress of Students, an international anti-
imperialist organization of Latin America. He joined a few other
Marxist leaders of Cuba to form the Communist Party in 1925.
The Communists worked to unite white and Afro-Cuban workers
from rural and urban areas. Later in 1925, Mella was 18 days into
a hunger strike against the US-supported Machado dictatorship
when he fled to México in response to assassination threats. He became a member of the Central Committee of the Communist Party

of México and wrote for *El Machete*, the party's newsletter. He also became general secretary of the Anti-imperialist League of the Americas and founder and leader of the Association of New Cuban Revolutionary Emigrants. Mella worked in solidarity with anti-imperialist movements across Latin America. He went to Brussels in 1927 to participate in the World Congress against Colonial Oppression and Imperialism and visited the Soviet Union. His leadership in critical global citizenship brought him many powerful enemies, and he was assassinated in México City on January 10, 1929, most likely on orders from Cuban dictator Gerardo Machado.

Mella's contribution to civic education and critical global citizenship in Cuba was far reaching. In 1923 he led the First National Congress of Students in efforts at meaningful reforms at the University of Havana. Later that year he proposed courses that advocated proletarian class struggle at the José Martí Popular University. His revolutionary leadership in the student movement influenced later student uprisings against the Machado and Batista dictatorships. The Revolution's triumph in 1959 owed much to the underground networks of student groups that were inspired by Mella's example (Hart, 2004).

Educational fronts and power struggles

The dictatorship of Gerardo Machado from 1925 to 1933 spawned a massive revolutionary opposition. He came to power by winning an election as the Liberal Party candidate, but he quickly turned his government into an authoritarian dictatorship. He was friendly to US businesses and grew a larger army to protect their interests. Machado extended his rule in 1928 for another six years without re-election. When the global economic depression hit Cuba, Machado did nothing to alleviate the increasing poverty. He repressed opposition movements with violence, and those movements in turn took to violent means. The *Directorio Estudiantil* [Student Directorate] regrouped after the assassination of Mella and went underground with a plan for violent attacks on the government. Another clandestine group called the ABC opposed Machado and US business but from a fascist position against Afro-

Cubans and communists (Pérez Cruz, 2001). Upon the inaugura-
tion of President Franklin D. Roosevelt in January 1933, the US
government ended its support for Machado. As a general strike
grew in the summer without intervention from US or Cuban
troops, Machado resigned and fled for the Bahamas before going to
the US to live.

The fall of Machado presented an opportunity for Cuba to
move in a progressive nationalist direction. US Ambassador Sum-
ner Welles approved the appointment of Carlos Manuel de
Céspedes as provisional president, but Cuba's military, militant
students, and revolutionary groups opposed this US choice. A revolt led by Sergeant Fulgencio Batista within weeks of the appointment overthrew Céspedes. Batista's dark skin worried many white
Cubans that he might bring favors to Afro-Cubans, but he publicly
rejected revolutionary student groups and took himself out of con-
sideration for appointment as provisional president. A junta of six
men ruled the country September 5 to 10, and Ambassador Welles,
describing the new leaders as "communistic," asked for a US military intervention. The junta chose Dr. Ramón Grau San Martín, a
physician and university professor who had supported the *Directorio
Estudiantil*, to be president. His government nationalized two mills
of the Cuban American Sugar Corporation as well as the Cuban
Electric Company. It also required that 50 percent of employees in
all enterprises be Cuban, alleviating fears that Spanish and Caribbean immigrants were taking jobs from native Cubans. The racism
against Haitian and Jamaican immigrants fueled these fears (Gott,
2004).

The Grau government managed to write a new constitution in
1933 that led to progressive changes. Women gained the right to
vote for the first time. Workers were granted an 8-hour day, a 44-
hour week, a month of paid vacation, and compulsory social insurance. Grau, however, was unable to control the conflicts among
fascist, conservative, reformist and socialist elements. Batista knew
that the US would support only a more conservative president, and
he convinced Carlos Mendieta, a leader of the fading Liberal Party,
to step forward as the new president on January 18, 1934. The US
government had never recognized Grau as president, but it en-

dorsed Mendieta within days of his takeover. Grau took exile in México. Convinced that its interests were secured, the US government abolished the Platt Amendment to appease Cuban nationalists. The US military base at Guantánamo Bay remained intact, though (Gott, 2004).

In March of 1934 Mendieta invited experts from the US to study conditions in Cuba and provide recommendations. The Foreign Policy Association, Inc., a non-governmental organization, assembled a team of 11 consultants from various backgrounds of expertise to act on the invitation. The educational expert was Lester McLean Wilson from Teachers College of Columbia University. The Association's report (1935) urged the Cuban government to address the health issues associated with rural poverty while facing the necessity for providing agricultural education to all rural children and adults. The lack of rural schools was a terrible problem, but the Association warned, "Practically nothing that the school might do can be effective unless rural home conditions can be changed" (p. 138).

Although Mendieta was president, Batista was the military strongman with real power. He led the Cuban military to transfer loyalty from Grau to Mendieta. When the socialist activist Antonio Guiteras Holmes revived a clandestine organization renamed Joven Cuba that precipitated general strikes, Batista and Mendieta imposed martial law and crushed the movement with arrests and torture. Guiteras was killed while he was planning to flee to México. The army came to dominate politics, and Batista used the tactics of Machado in repressing dissent (Gott, 2004).

Batista manipulated power struggles behind the scenes, and Cuba had a series of seven short-lived presidencies from 1934 to 1940 (Gott, 2004). When Batista sent soldiers to rural areas in 1936 to build schools and teach in them, President Miguel Mariano Gómez opposed the move as a troublesome measure of populism. The president's efforts to end the program resulted in his impeachment and termination, and his vice president took over. Batista formed an alliance of convenience with the communists in the *Partido Unión Revolucionaria* [Revolutionary Union Party]. They gained permission to organize legally, and he gained their support for his political ambitions, which was lacking from all other parties. Cuban resistance to government corruption grew until a 1939 assembly wrote a new constitution, which took affect in 1940. It included 13 articles regarding education and culture. Article 49 provided adult education and a commitment to end illiteracy. Article 51 promoted the development of patriotism, solidarity, and democracy in education. Nationalist themes appeared in Article 55, which required regulation of private schools, and Article 56, which provided a distinctly Cuban education in literature, history, geography, and civics.

Batista finally had his chance to govern officially when he was elected president in 1940. During World War II, Cuba provided air and naval bases for the US. Batista legalized the Communist Party in 1943 and established diplomatic relations with the Soviet Union, which was allied with the US in the war. High sugar prices brought a healthy economy, and many Cubans later associated Batista with years of prosperity. In 1944 Batista supported the presidential campaign of his prime minister, Carlos Saladrigas, but the victory went to the return of Grau San Martín, this time representing middle-class interests in the *Auténtico* [Authentic] Party. As the Cold War emerged, Grau moved against the Communist Party and the union it dominated, the *Confederación de Trabajadores de Cuba* [Federation of Cuban Workers]. The *Auténticos* won again in 1948, when Carlos Prío Socarrás defeated the leftist Eduardo Chibás of the *Partido Revolucionario Cubano Ortodoxo* [Cuban Revolutionary Party-Orthodox]. Prío's four-year administration became known as the most corrupt and violent in Cuba's history as a republic (Gott, 2004).

Education in Cuba during the 1940s became more polarized along political fronts. The pro-fascist organization *Pro Patria y Escuela* [For Country and School] formed in 1941. The *Federación de Maestros Cubanos* [Federation of Cuban Teachers], officially accepted by the Batista administration in 1942, joined other organizations of public employees in solidarity against fascism as World War II escalated. The Communist Party of Cuba changed its name in 1944 to *Partido Socialista Popular* (PSP), and Juan Marinello, a teacher and elected representative of the party, became Cuba's leading voice for ending illiteracy. As ideologies competed for the attention of Cuban educators, the pragmatism of John Dewey prevailed (Pérez Cruz, 2001). The "New School" followed US designs, and the University of Havana promoted the status quo. Illiteracy for Cubans over age 10 was at 22.1 percent in 1943, and there was no established plan among policymakers to eliminate it.

Ana Moya de Perea conducted an analysis of illiteracy in Cuba that appeared in *Bohemia*, a popular Cuban periodical on news and culture, in 1949 (Pérez Cruz, 2001). She denounced neocononialism and proposed a national campaign to eliminate illiteracy. The bourgeois elite of Cuba, though, loyal to the continuing political and economic hegemony of the US, never acted on the provision in the Constitution of 1940 for ending illiteracy. Rural populations suffered the most, and *campesinos* who were illiterate were powerless to effect change in a system that exploited their labor and denied them land. Their only hope was for a revolutionary change to bring their voices to power.

Revolutionary struggle and the role of education

Batista, facing the likelihood of not being elected president, returned to power as dictator on March 10, 1952, in a bloodless coup with military support. The Truman Administration welcomed Batista's new rule with military and economic aid, and Eisenhower continued the support. Cubans, disgusted by the corruption of democratically-elected leaders, seemed to accept the new dictatorship. The exceptional skepticism came from a group of university students and the Orthodox Party, and Fidel Castro was a member of the latter.

Castro's father, Angel Castro, was an immigrant from Spain who married Lina Ruz, a woman from the western Cuban province of Pinar del Rio (Gott, 2004). They had several children, and Angel became a wealthy landowner in the eastern province of Oriente. Among Fidel's siblings only his younger brother Raul would play an important role in the Revolution. Fidel graduated from the law school at the University of Havana in 1950 and was a candidate for

Congress in 1952 until Batista's coup. After the coup, he gathered several of his revolutionary friends from the university and began making plans for transforming Cuba.

Just four days after the coup, a group of students issued the *Declaration of principals of the Federation of University Students* (Hart, 2004). It was then published in *Bohemia* within two weeks. The document demanded a return to a constitutional republic "free of foreign interference and national falsification" (p. 68). University students had been at the forefront to oppose Machado's dictatorship, and a new generation of students became a catalyst to build a revolutionary movement against Batista. Castro was not among this student group, but he soon was making plans to overtake Batista by force.

July 26, 1953 is the date most celebrated by Cubans who identify with the Revolution. On that date Castro led an armed group of about 100 rebels in a surprise attack on the Moncada army barracks in Santiago. The army drove the rebels away after killing and capturing many, and Castro escaped but was arrested days later. A black lieutenant took Castro to the police station in Santiago rather than Moncada, where he likely would have been executed as had been the case with other rebels held there (Gott, 2004).

Castro's trial in September was the setting of his most famous speech, which was later published under the title *History will absolve me*. It gave details of 'five revolutionary laws' that would have gone into effect had the revolt succeeded. First, a revival of the Constitution of 1940 would set the stage for all other changes. Second, the state would grant property to renting farmers while compensating former owners based on rent they would have received over 10 years. Third, all workers in major industries would share 30 percent of all profits. Fourth, sugar planters would share 55 percent of the profits of their production. Fifth, the state would confiscate all assets gained from the corruption of previous regimes and would redistribute the wealth for workers' retirement, hospitals, and charitable organizations. In addition to these five laws, Castro (1968) expressed the need for Cuba's solidarity with the people throughout the Americas, ensuring that "those politically persecuted by bloody tyrants oppressing our sister nations would find generous asylum, brotherhood and bread in the land of Martí" (p. 45). Another part of the speech claimed that education would become a right of all Cuban citizens, that rural education would be introduced where necessary, and that teachers' pay would be raised substantially in all schools. Altogether, the speech documented the expression of critical global citizenship among Cuban revolutionaries of that time.

While in prison, Castro conducted courses in philosophy, world history, political economy and speech for other prisoners (Gott, 2004). Castro and 27 others who attacked Moncada received sentences of up to 15 years, but popular pressure on the Batista regime led to their release along with over 200 political prisoners on May 15, 1955. Within a month, the July 26 Movement (M-26) emerged, uniting *Moncadistas*, members of the Orthodox Party, and members of the Revolutionary National Movement, an anti-Batista organization formed in early 1953. Within another month, Castro was in México to begin preparing for an insurrection against Batista. There he welcomed the participation of Ernesto 'Ché' Guevara, the Argentine doctor who had left Guatemala after the US helped a military coup overthrow the democratically-elected leftist Arbenz government. Also among the rebels in training was Castro's brother, Raúl.

In August 1956, the Federation of University Students signed the México Pact with the M-26 to declare their mutual goals and strategies for overthrowing Batista (Gott, 2004). On November 25, 1956, Fidel and Raúl Castro, along with Guevara and 79 other rebel combatants crowded onto the small yacht *Granma* and landed at Las Coloradas in Belic, Oriente, near the eastern end of Cuba, on December 2. The first battle against Batista's troops occurred three days later, and half of the rebels were either killed or captured and imprisoned. Guevara was among the wounded.

The rebels regrouped and fought their way through several victorious battles in the mountainous Sierra Maestra region with the support of M-26 activists and insurgents of the plains. As territories in the mountains became liberated, the growing Rebel Army conducted literacy drives. Initiated by Che Guevara, these drives used books donated by supporters from nearby cities and brought literacy to members of the Rebel Army as well as *campesinos*. These efforts became the most immediate antecedents to the National Literacy Campaign of 1961 (Hart, 2004).

In November 1957, rebel leaders issued a document titled *Elements for integrating the school program for the troops* (Pérez Cruz, 2001). It directed the combatants to learn Cuban history and geography, material conditions that affected the lives of Cuban people, progressive thoughts of liberators, objectives and problems of the Cuban Revolution, and the challenges presented by the counter-revolution within Cuba and from the US. A course on ethics would use texts from Martí, the 1940 Constitution, and the Universal Declaration of Human Rights.

The Rebel Army protected new schools while Batista's army bombed mountain populations indiscriminately. They camouflaged the schools and built them underground to protect the *campesinos'* children. Many of these families had never been in a school. Although the latest national census of 1953 placed illiteracy at 23.6 percent, a 1957 study by a Catholic organization, *Agrupación Católica Universitaria* [University Catholic Group], found that in rural populations 43 percent of adults were illiterate and 44 percent had never attended a school (Pérez Cruz, 2001).

Education had a central position in the ideological struggle against Batista, who identified with private schools that were mostly Catholic. The ultraconservative tradition of the Spanish clergy had influenced the Cuban clergy. The Rebel Army promoted education for all – black and white, rich and poor, male and female – in the *Mambí* tradition, and Batista's regime promoted the status quo with a plan called *Punto IV*, which trained and rewarded teachers on the ideology of US hegemony. Juan Marinello distributed a PSP underground pamphlet denouncing the government's complicity with US imperialism. Meanwhile, the Catholic clergy, using anti-communist rhetoric, became more vocal in support of Batista's education plan with the slogan "One School with God," and the declaration that Cuba would govern with "the Christian morality" (Pérez Cruz, 2001).

C. Fred Judson (1984) wrote of the political education that inspired the Rebel Army through extremely adverse conditions in the mountains of the Sierra Maestra region. His main theme, based on

Georges Sorel's theory of revolutionary myth, is that the Rebel Army became the myth, or heroic legend, that incorporated the myths of national redemption developed historically by the *Mambí*, Maceo, Martí, Mella, and other heroes. This myth, established through the difficult process of gaining the trust and cooperation of the *campesinos*, was established with growing victories against Batista's army. The Rebel Army's original members were mainly urban, privileged young men, and they became genuine revolutionaries by working side by side with *campesinos* and by learning directly of their struggles to survive. Batista's army had forced *campesinos* to forfeit land for *latifundistas* [elite landowners], and *campesinos* needed time before they were able to trust the Rebel Army.

Judson (1984) defines political education as "the taking on (passive) or inculcation (active) of values, attitudes or ideology pertaining to the political sphere of human existence," with the word 'political' implying "power and its use for human ends, however diverse" (p. 7, Judson's parenthetic notes). He emphasizes the experiential nature of the Rebel Army's political education. Enduring the elements of the mountains, the danger from air attacks, the discipline needed to deal decisively with enemy informants and deserters – these events often were impossible to anticipate and required immediate actions for which there were no formal preparations. These challenges tested the revolutionary will of the combatants.

By the summer of 1958, the growing Rebel Army had built strong momentum against Batista's army, even though the latter still had many times more soldiers. Raúl Castro's column of troops formed the Jose Martí School for Troop Instruction at Tumbasiete, Oriente, which became a model for the *Fuerzas Armadas Revolucionarias* [Revolutionary Armed Forces] after the triumph of the Revolution. Recruits in the column had three months to study topics about Cuba, including history, geography, economics, civics, Martí, and specific problems/objectives of the Cuban Revolution. The staff at the school created its own text for the history of Cuba, presenting Marxist interpretations without explicitly using the name of Marxism. Graduates of the school led courses of "civic education" when they returned to their units. They also served as moderators in local labor disputes. Years later, many testified to the important

role that the Tumbasiete school had in creating revolutionary conscience throughout the most critical years of the early 1960s
(Judson, 1984).

   The *Mambí* educational tradition prevailed over the exclusion-
ary status quo as the Revolutionary forces triumphed. Education
fueled and was fueled by the Cuban Revolution. Internationalism
for uniting Latin America was an important theme in Cuba's struggle for authentic independence, and Cuba's form of critical global
citizenship defied the US as it had Spain. Literacy drives advanced
the Revolutionary struggle, and the victorious revolutionary government would continue to give literacy a central priority. As Batista fled Cuba on January 1, 1959, the educational work of the
Revolution had barely begun.

3. Literacy and Citizenship for a New Cuba, 1959-1960

As Cuba's new revolutionary government took power in January 1, 1959, it was not clear how Cuba would change or how the rest of the world would accept the changes. The Cold War was getting colder after the Soviet Union was first to enter outer space in 1957. The US government was not going to tolerate a socialist nation in the Americas but was willing to wait and see how far Cuba would take reforms. The CIA's support in the 1954 military coup that ousted Guatemala's democratically elected leftist president, Jacobo Arbenz, was recent evidence that the US government would use force to protect its economic interests in Latin America. People in revolutionary Cuba were participants in a new critical global citizenship in regard to their nation's relations with the US and the rest of Latin America and the "Third World."

Che Guevara (2003) captured the internationalism of the new revolutionary government in a speech on January 29, 1959. First he spoke of the Rebel Army implementing the agrarian reforms that came from the ideas of the peasants as their zones were liberated during the war. Then he urged all Cubans to be prepared to become a guerrilla army in order to defend the Revolution along with the Rebel Army. He ended with a plea for all Latin American nations: "Finally, we must open new roads identifying our common interests as underdeveloped nations. We must be aware of all efforts to divide us and struggle against those who try to sow the seeds of discord among us" (p. 95).

The early provisional government moved quickly to establish a new order. With overwhelming popular support and after providing varying degrees of due process, it executed several hundred Cubans who were held responsible for atrocities under Batista's rule (Farber, 1976). The results of the non-revolutionary aftermath of Cuba's 1933 revolution likely informed the decision to use swift and severe punishment against Batistiano criminals. Castro's July 26th Movement laid claim to exclusive rights in ruling the provisional

government. The only challenge among other revolutionary organizations was from the university students in the Directorio Revolucionario [Revolutionary Directorate]. Days after the triumph of the
Revolution, they stole weapons from a military post. Cubans overwhelmingly denounced this bold move, and the student group dis-
solved quickly.

Castro in a speech in 1974 explained the urgency of the provisional government: "We had to seize revolutionary power; we had
to begin to make the Revolution. And, the only way to do that was
by taking the state and establishing a revolutionary government"
(quoted in Roman, 2003, p. 62). Raúl Castro in another 1974
speech explained why the provisional government could not include
representative institutions: "At the time we did not have a strong
party, the mass organizations were not sufficiently developed...To
all these factors we should add a certain lack of experience and understanding...regarding the importance of these representative institutions" (quoted in Roman, 2003, p. 62).

The victorious revolutionaries named Manuel Urrutia as president and José Miró Cardona as prime minister on January 2. The
US government officially recognized the new Cuban government
on January 7, after much of Western Europe had done so. Many
Cubans who identified with Batista fled for the US, and on January
16 Cuba asked the US government to return "war criminals" and
the money taken by Batista from the treasury. The New York
Times reported on February 11 that the US military, which had
trained Batista's army, was withdrawing from Cuba with the exception of the naval base at Guantánamo (Franklin, 1997). Miró resigned as prime minister on February 13, and Fidel Castro took his
place.

Education under the new revolutionary government

The new Cuban government wasted no time in bringing
changes to education. Armando Hart Dávalos, a lawyer who had
been active in the urban revolutionary underground during the
war, became Minister of Education. Under his leadership the revolutionary government took its first steps to formulate the National

Literacy Campaign early in 1959. Hart declared the initiation of the Urgent Plan of Cuban Literacy on February 17. When asked in an interview in February in what form the literacy plan would be realized, Hart responded that it "will involve the decided cooperation of the people through civic institutions, worker organizations, live classes, and volunteers, in order to carry the interest and desire to learn reading and writing to the most remote corners of Cuba." (Torroella, 1959, p. 39, my translation) In March, the Ministry of Education created the National Commission of Literacy and Functional Education (CNAEF), which began work on a comprehensive plan for the elimination of illiteracy.

The Ministry faced a great challenge. Like so many "Third World" nations, Cuba had a history of widely neglected education. The last national census taken before 1959 was in 1953, and it reported an illiteracy rate for Cuba as a whole at 23.6 percent. The rural rate was much higher. That same census found that 64 percent of children within the age range of compulsory education were not attending school. It also discovered that only three percent of those attending were completing the compulsory requirement (MacDonald, 1985). Many rural zones lacked schools, and those with schools often lacked certified teachers. Universities were accessible only to privileged elite who chose overwhelmingly to study the lucrative fields of business and law while rejecting scientific courses needed to bring Cuba out of underdevelopment.

A new revolutionary hegemony depended not only on the elimination of illiteracy but also on the support of universities. Castro declared on March 15 that universities needed to be organized nationally to prepare professionals for the Revolution and for the development of Cuba, but a debate followed over whether the University of Havana should remain independent from the Revolution. Guevara, in a speech on university reform and revolution on October 17, 1959, asserted that the deciding factor of this debate was the grand majority of Cubans who were enthusiastic about making the Revolution (MacDonald, 1985). In the same month students organized the José Antonio Echeverría University Student Brigades to bring the same argument to the debate.

The conflict over the university escalated in mid-1960, and the government fired faculty who were identified as counter-revolutionary. The Popular Socialist Party (PSP), the Federation of University Students (FEU), and Minister of Education Armando Hart were instrumental in pressuring the government toward this policy. The government and the PSP agreed that university faculty need not be communist but that they must be dedicated to serving the Revolution. Students opposed to the Revolution's movement toward socialism formed the Revolutionary Student Directorate (DRE). They lacked university support, and many joined counter-revolutionary organizations in Cuba or among exiles in Miami (Suchlicki, 1969).

Another great priority was the creation of elementary and secondary schools for all Cubans. Castro approved the opening of 10,000 new classrooms nationwide. An acute shortage of teachers for the new classrooms was the result of many middle-class teachers having fled the Revolution for Miami. Youth with a high school education became provisional teachers to bridge the gap. Castro declared that every school would be a fortress for the Revolution, and many military posts from Batista's army became schools (Pérez Cruz, 2001). Education clearly became a greater priority than militarization. Ideas would become the primary weapons for defending the Revolution.

The first records of literacy drives in the Cuban provinces appeared in September of 1959 (Pérez Cruz, 2001). The CNAEF reported the nation's totals as 844 literacy centers, 19,075 students becoming literate, and 2,832 literacy teachers. These efforts were taking place mainly in the rural areas where literacy rates were the lowest. They were part of a comprehensive program to bring improvements in infrastructure, health care, and education to the neediest parts of Cuba.

On December 23 the Revolutionary government took a bold step toward taking the schools away from the hegemony of the elite by enacting Law 680 in the spirit of the 1940 Constitutional provisions for education. This law provided a central place in grades six and higher for a curriculum based on the humanist, nationalist, anti-imperialist ideals of Martí. It rejected the traditional schooling of passive learning and promoted an education that responded directly to the specific needs of Cuban children and adolescents. John Dewey had been a member of the American Anti-Imperialist League, and his ideas of student-centered education contributed to Cuba's educational front against imperialism.

While the needs of Cuban youth were addressed, there were also the needs of the nation. The curriculum for science at all levels had never received a high priority before the Revolution since the development of Cuba for Cubans had not been a priority of colonial and neocolonial governments. The elite were disproportionately from the cities, and rural education was substandard wherever it existed. The revolutionary government encouraged prospective teachers to become science instructors and recruited 1,000 new teachers for rural schools (Pérez Cruz, 2001).

Land redistribution and US reactions

These educational changes took place along with another revolutionary development with high priority—agrarian reform. The Agrarian Reform Law, based on Castro's ideas from *History will absolve me*, went into effect in May 1959. This law placed a 966-acre limit on the size of farms and a 3,300-acre limit for cattle ranches, breaking up the large landholdings (*latifundia*), including sugar properties owned by US companies (DeFronzo, 2007). The new commitments to rural education worked with the redistribution of land to help bridge the large gulf between the urban and rural populations. The National Institute for Agricultural Reform (INRA) was formed to coordinate efforts in support of the new rural cultural and educational programs.

The *latifundia* system disappeared, and *campesinos* suddenly became owners of the land they worked. The government provided fixed prices for their produce along with low-interest loans. Seasonal workers gained full-time employment, and salaries increased. "People's stores" brought inexpensive goods to rural areas. State farms were considered to be the most productive and socially beneficial, followed by cooperatives. The government allowed small private farmers to keep their land, and they were the only significant remnant of the private sector in Cuba (Benjamin, Collins & Scott, 2003).

June was a pivotal month. The revolutionary government knew that its land reforms meant relations with the US would likely become troubled. The Agrarian Reform Law was implemented on June 3, and two days later US Senator George Smathers, a Democrat of Florida, proposed a bill that would reduce the quota of Cuban sugar. The US government protested that Cuba's basis for compensating US landowners was based on tax assessment rates that had not been changed in 30 or 40 years. This allowed these landowners to pay very low taxes for decades, and suddenly they wanted an adjusted assessment in their favor regarding compensation. In the following years the Cuban government negotiated settlements with landowners and governments of Britain, Canada, France, Italy, México, Spain, and Sweden, but such efforts with the US remained unresolved (Franklin, 1997).

These reforms became immensely popular with *campesinos*. Castro promised them in June that their children would have schools, sports facilities, and health care (Gott, 2004). The revolutionary government clearly announced that peasants would no longer be regarded as second-class citizens, and thousands of them went to Havana by horseback or bus to hear Castro speak to commemorate the Moncada uprising on July 26. Lázaro Cárdenas, the revolutionary president of México in the 1930s, appeared next to Castro to express his solidarity.

President Urrutia's entire cabinet initially had approved the land reform law, but several of its members began to oppose the reforms, calling them 'communistic' (Gott, 2004). They joined Urrutia in calling themselves 'anti-communists' in opposition to what they saw as a Castro-led movement toward communism. Many of those in such opposition were large landholders who began to feel that their fortunes were threatened. After Urrutia made his opposition known in published interviews, Castro forced him to resign and chose a lawyer named Osvaldo Dorticós to replace him. Dorticós had been secretary to Juan Marinello, the long-time leader of the Communist Party.

The old Cuban elite also felt threatened by the way Castro was declaring an end to racial discrimination. Castro's July 26 Movement had not embraced racial equality openly the way the Communist Party had, but Castro began to speak of the Revolution's need for racial equality and unity in March 1959. He opposed and even closed down black separatist movements while emphasizing the importance of promoting a Revolution free of racial antagonisms. In regard to anti-racism Castro was no more progressive than Kennedy (Gott, 2004). Although the Revolution brought new horizons for economic progress to Afro-Cubans, there was a long history of discrimination that would not easily be transformed.

Around the world people showed great interest in the Cuban Revolution, but the greatest stakeholders were Cuba's neighbors in the US and Latin America. US sugar and fruit companies had economic interests in their large Cuban land holdings. Latin American leftist intellectuals saw Cuba as a pioneer nation with great possibilities for progressive change. Castro knew that the US government would oppose not only the land reforms but also the prospect of other Latin American nations following Cuba's example in leftist revolution. It is not known exactly when Castro decided to pursue a Marxist-Leninist centralized state, but the reasoning behind it apparently included the anticipation that it would be necessary for countering the inevitable US reaction against Cuba's political and economic changes (DeFronzo, 2007).

Sugar accounted for over 80 percent of Cuban exports, and most of it went to the United States. US-owned companies controlled nine of Cuba's ten largest sugar mills and 12 of the next 20 in size, and overall these companies accounted for nearly 40 percent of Cuba's sugar production (Wolf, 1969; DeFronzo, 2007). US companies also had large investments in utilities, manufacturing, mining, and oil refineries. The US government came under increasing pressure to protect these economic interests as the Cuban government moved forward with revolutionary land redistribution.

Counter-revolutionary forces directed and armed by the CIA made efforts to sabotage the progress by late 1959 (Escalante, 1995). Activity of counter-revolutionary bands grew in the beginning of 1960 in the mountains of the Escambray region of South-

Central Cuba. The Cuban government looked to Europe for arms to defend the Revolution. On March 4, a ship named "La Coubre" was carrying arms purchased by Cuba from the government in Belgium into the harbor of Havana when it exploded. The disaster, attributed to the CIA, left 72 dead and 200 wounded. Castro reiterated Cuba's need to secure arms for defending the Revolution, and he used a phrase that has become a popular slogan: "*Patria o Muerte*" [Homeland or death].

President Eisenhower directed the CIA on March 17 to begin a secret mission to train anti-Castro Cuban exiles in Guatemala for a future invasion of Cuba. Continued by Kennedy, this mission culminated in the Bay of Pigs attack in April 1961. In April 1960 Cuban Foreign Minister Raúl Roa García stated that Guatemala was conspiring to invade Cuba. The Guatemalan government denied it and cut diplomatic ties with Cuba. On May 7 Cuba re-opened diplomatic relations with the Soviet Union, which had been severed in 1952 after Batista's coup (Franklin, 1997).

The CIA was troubled by Castro's popularity and plotted to undermine his credibility before moving on to assassination attempts (Select Committee to Study Governmental Operations with Respect to Intelligence Activities, 2003). There were plans in early 1960 to spray Castro's studio with a chemical that produced effects similar to LSD, but this idea was rejected when studies revealed that the chemical was unreliable. Another plan involved lacing Castro's cigars with a chemical that produced disorientation, but it is not known whether these treated cigars ever reached his hands. On August 16, 1960, the CIA gave an official a box of Castro's favorite cigars with instructions to treat them with a deadly poison. The official confirmed that the cigars were ready on October 7. There is no record as to whether an attempt was made to pass the cigars to Castro. Another CIA plot in August involved recruiting criminals of illegal gambling operations to assassinate Castro. One plan to poison Castro's drinking water proceeded to the point of paying a Cuban accomplice a probable amount of $10,000 in advance, but the dissolving pills were potent for a limited time.

The United States also used economic means to subvert the Revolution. In June of 1960, US citizens who owned oil refineries in Cuba refused to refine crude oil from the Soviet Union. On July 5, 1960, the US boycott of Cuban sugar was announced. On August 6, the revolutionary government declared the nationalization of its oil refineries, in addition to its telephone and electric services. These had all been owned by US monopolies. These events marked the beginning of a new trading partnership: Cuban sugar for oil from the Soviet Union. As Nixon and Kennedy campaigned for president, each tried to exceed the other in expressing concern about Cuba's ties to Moscow.

Literacy and internationalism in Russian and Chinese Revolutions

Although Cuba's government did not declare the socialist nature of the Revolution until April of 1961, the US government viewed Cuba as a communist threat in the Cold War well before that time. Anti-communism had become so ingrained in the mainstream world view of Cubans that the July 26 Movement was in no hurry to declare the Revolution as socialist. The world had seen triumphant Marxist revolutions in Russia and China, and the Korean War had ended in a stalemate. Lenin and Mao were not educational theorists, but both wrote about the central role of education in transforming a society in a proletarian revolution. Both also wrote of internationalism as a key to a successful transition.

Marx (1906) wrote of education that it must combine work, study and physical education in order to bring the working class out of a life of alienating manual labor and into possibilities for human completeness. This comprehensive education would contribute "not only as one of the methods of adding to the proficiency of production, but as the only method of producing fully developed human beings" (p. 530). Marx saw capitalist schooling as a tool for reproducing class divisions between capitalist and wage laborer, and he asserted that only a socialist society could transform education into a mechanism for empowering all people.

Prior to Russia's October 1917 Socialist Revolution, 73 percent of the adult population was illiterate (Kumanev, 1970). Lenin asserted that no communist society could be constructed with an illiterate population, and combating illiteracy became an immediate priority in the Revolution. Native languages other than Russian received equal status throughout the country, and writing was introduced to languages that had had none. The Congress created schools for illiterate youth and adults, and Lenin issued a decree in 1919 directing all people from age 8 to 50 who could not read or write to attend such schools for three or four months. Workdays were reduced two hours without reducing pay in order to make time for this literacy campaign. Since professional teachers were in short supply for this national project, the decree enlisted all literate people to contribute to instruction. The Red Army also conducted schools for eliminating illiteracy among its troops. Youth from the Young Communist League participated widely in instruction, and they moved to teach in rural regions with the greatest need. An estimated 2.7 million adults learned to read and write in 1920.

Lenin spoke of literacy alone not being enough (Kumanev, 1970). He envisioned a state of the Bolshevik Party that promoted mass literacy as a means for elevating levels of culture and industrial production. He emphasized the need to develop science from its most advanced European and American manifestations. As Lenin's health began to fail in 1922, he continued to place more resources into education. The campaign to abolish illiteracy continued well after his death. Stalin's rise to megalomaniac power, against which Lenin forewarned, led to Russia's development of a privileged bureaucracy and abandonment of internationalist socialism.

Mao Zedong believed that the entire revolutionary movement in China could be summed up as an educational movement and that the goal of education was to help establish the new China as socialist (Chu, 1980; Hawkins, 1974). He saw education as essential in replacing a dictatorship of the bourgeoisie with a dictatorship of the proletariat and in achieving the ultimate goal of a communist society. Mao saw in China's poverty the preconditions to revolution, and in its undereducated masses the opportunity to teach new ideas. As early as 1927, he led Chinese communists in establishing schools for children of peasants. He made a priority of spreading literacy among the troops of the Red Army and among general adult populations. Upon the 1949 triumph of the Chinese Revolution, education became part of the struggle to eliminate the ideol-

ogy of private ownership and means of production and to promote
the new ideology of proletarian dictatorship. The term *re-education*
described how educated Chinese faced a new ideology and system.
Many educated youth experienced this by learning how to work in
the fields in order to contribute to the most immediate needs for
feeding people.

Mao's anti-imperialist views were moved by a memory from his
childhood in which he saw a sign on the gate of Shanghai International Park reading "Chinese and dogs are not allowed" (Chu,
1980). He saw the Opium War of 1840 as a turning point that
made China a semi-colonial and semi-feudal society under alternat-
ing regimes of Japanese and Western powers. Mao wrote extensively after 1949 about the need for an internationalist education to
unite Asian, African, and Latin American peoples in Marxism
against imperialist powers. He envisioned a China that would learn
from other cultures while critically guarding against unwanted foreign influences. In 1954 the Central Government issued mandates
that all education must contribute to the development of patriotism
and internationalism.

Xiaodong Niu (1994) wrote of similarities between John Dewey
and Mao regarding education despite their different cultures and
societies. Both linked education to democracy, although only Mao
placed class struggle at the center of democracy. Mao believed that
a new democracy could emerge only after a proletarian dictatorship
assumed power. Mao, like Dewey, promoted learner-centered instruction. Both insisted that education cannot be an imposition
from teachers onto students but rather must be a mechanism to
foster students' independent learning. Mao favored the direct involvement of schools in the rural and urban workplaces, and Dewey
wrote extensively about the need to connect students' experiences
in real-world problem solving. Both changed the way teachers
worked in their respective societies.

Latin American Marxism and education

The previous chapter included the historical development of
Marxism in Cuba. US citizens commonly do not understand that

Latin American Marxism has rich traditions that began long before
the triumph of the Cuban Revolution in 1959 (Abendroth, 2005).
Marxism in Latin America never was an imitation of European or
Asian Marxism. Latin America had its own historical development
with regard to colonialism and racism, and its manifestations of
Marxism are unique.

Class exploitation in Latin America has imperialist and racist
roots. The spectrum of power went from European privilege to indigenous and African slavery. Spain and Portugal originally sought
gold in the Americas and later turned to silver, sugar, and tobacco
for mercantilist wealth. The exploitation of slave labor generated
tremendous material wealth for the empires, but the triumphant
slave uprising of the Haitian Revolution against French colonizers
in 1804 provoked fear that slaves elsewhere could do the same.

Most colonies of Latin America gained national independence
in the early 1820s, but Cuba, along with Puerto Rico, was an exception as it remained a Spanish colony until 1898. Nationals who
prospered under colonialism continued to exercise economic and
political control. Wealthy landowners in the *latifundio* system hired
caudillos to lead mercenary militias in keeping landless *campesinos*
subservient. The passing of slavery gave way to debt peonage for
many workers.

The United States issued the Monroe Doctrine in 1823 to declare that newly independent countries in Latin America could
never again fall under the control of European nations. This allowed the United States to pursue its own economic and political
interests among its vulnerable neighbors to the South. U.S. interventions in Latin America consistently and often violently have sti-
fled democratic movements for social justice, true national sovereignty, and grassroots economic development.

The October Revolution of Russia in 1917 triggered the Red
Scare in the United States but also inspired many movements
against economic exploitation around the globe, including some in
the United States. Socialist organizations throughout Latin America grew significantly. Two leaders, in addition to Cuba's Julio Antonio Mella among many others, who helped to shape the early

development of Latin American Marxism were Aníbal Ponce of Argentina, and José Mariátegui of Perú.

Aníbal Ponce (1898-1938), an Argentine psychologist who wrote extensively on education, became an influential voice of the recent history of Latin America. He emphasized the importance of culture in his advocacy of Marxism. He wrote boldly in support of anti-imperialist campaigns throughout Latin America and joined the Mexican League of Revolutionary Writers and Artists while in exile.

Argentina in Ponce's time experienced economic and political turmoil. The end of the 19th Century brought a growing criticism against economic liberalism, and an emerging labor movement troubled the far right that had strong ties to the Catholic Church and the capitalist class (McGee Deutsch, 1999). This rightist movement marginalized immigrants and Jews. It attributed the 1890 depression to Jewish international capital. The National Autonomist Party rose to power while upholding the national oligarchy's interests. The media blamed immigrants while ignoring the struggles of the working and middle classes. Anarchists organized a general strike in 1902, but the media targeted immigrants as the instigators. As a result, the xenophobic Congress passed a harsh residence law. A reactionary movement grew in response to the growing labor movement. Police and workers clashed in retaliatory attacks in 1909, and Congress passed laws to halt the entrance of leftist foreigners and to stifle the proletarian movement. In 1919 a large general strike battled with rightist paramilitary forces that received weapons and support from the military. The *Liga Patriótica Argentina* became the central organization of elitists in the 1920s, influencing the government with its ideology that upheld conservative concepts of Catholicism and morality while aggressively opposing the labor movement.

Ponce (1975) analyzed education from a Marxist perspective through the ages from what he called 'primitive communities' to the contemporary bourgeois social order. He wrote that bourgeois educators like Winetka, Howard, Dalton, and Montessori left out the issues of class while searching for ways to transform society. Ponce confronted the middle class for accepting these educational developments instead of uniting with the struggles of the working class. He claimed that bourgeois schools, in service to the ruling class, would never allow proletarian interests to gain significant representation. Ponce claimed that bourgeois society, along with its schools, was approaching fascism and that proletarian class struggle was necessary throughout society. Schools, he added, could contribute to such struggle along methodological and doctrinal fronts. Ponce's methodological front advocated more emphasis on collective work instead of individualism in reforms for increased student freedom. His doctrinal front called for a curriculum that supported proletarian interest, claiming that the myth of the neutral educator served only to perpetuate the social relations of class exploitation.

Ponce's arguments are significant to the role of civic education in the Cuban Revolution (Ponce, 1975; Abendroth, 2005). The National Literacy Campaign succeeded in 1961 because it followed the Revolution's 1959 triumph. Conversely, the Revolution likely would not have survived without the success of the Literacy Campaign. It was a campaign with revolutionary methodological and doctrinal fronts. The urgent call for all citizens to collaborate in the movement to eliminate illiteracy gave the methodological front its edge. The doctrinal front involved content that exposed the oppression of colonial and neocolonial Cuba and that highlighted the vision for emancipation through projects of the Revolution.

José Mariátegui (1895-1930) is perhaps the most widely known Marxist of Latin America from the first half of the 20th Century. Raised in a poor family, he taught himself journalism before studying in Europe and declaring himself a Marxist. He was able to go to Europe because the Leguía dictatorship offered him a choice in 1920 between jail and exile to Europe. He returned to Perú in 1923 and became a spokesperson for the American Revolutionary Popular Alliance Party. In 1928 he left that party due to its reformist platform and founded the Peruvian Socialist Party. Mariátegui's (1971) *Seven interpretive essays on Peruvian reality*, published originally in 1928 in Lima, contained essays that had been published in journals. The themes pertained to all of Latin America. They included pre- and post-independence economic exploitation, a small elite's oppressive possession of land, and the forced slavery of native peoples and Africans. The Leguía dictatorship ignored or tolerated Mariátegui's writings until his newspaper *Labor* led to his arrest in 1927 and his house being raided in 1929. Mariátegui stirred controversy mostly with his ideas of how ethnicity, nationalism and class were interrelated. He opposed the Moscow-based Third Communist International (Comintern) in its position that indigenous peoples and oppressed ethnic groups should form their own nations. When the Comintern applied this idea to Latin America, Mariátegui countered that the real solution was the abolition of the land tenure system through socialist revolution. He believed that a separate state for indigenous people in South America would only result in an Indian bourgeois state with new forms of economic exploitation from the outside and from within. He also asserted that citizenship in such a state would be difficult to determine due to Perú's large population of *mestizos*. Although not Native American, Mariátegui knew the historic and current nationalist struggles by indigenous peoples in South America and advocated a movement for their interests and for those of all working and landless people. His arguments became a central part of discussions in Buenos Aires at the first Continental Congress of Latin American Communist Parties in 1929 (Becker, 2003). The struggle uniting issues of ethnicity, nationalism, and class continues in the Zapatistas of Chiapas, México and in parts of Central America and the Andes.

Ponce and Mariátegui represent the early Marxism of Latin America that is unknown to the vast majority of US citizens. Although never a self-acclaimed Marxist, Augusto César Sandino played an important role in leading an anti-imperialist guerilla war against the US military occupation of Nicaragua from 1927 to 1933. A right-wing military dictatorship prevailed in Nicaragua for four decades, but the 1979 armed overthrow of Somoza claimed Sandino's name as the Sandinista National Liberation Front. Latin America's struggles against US imperialism began well before the Cuban Revolution. One cannot understand the Cuban Revolution without historical knowledge of prior US economic and political penetrations in Nicaragua, México, Guatemala, and Cuba itself. Only a critical global citizenship can cut through the dominant ver-

sion of history that tends to glorify all US foreign interventions of
the past and present.

Cuba's new internationalism and critical global citizenship

Cuba became a key player in the developments of the Cold
War as the 1962 Cuban Missile Crisis, known in Cuba as the October Crisis, would attest. There were many developments in the
years 1959 and 1960 that contributed to Cuba's transformation
from a republic dominated by the US to a revolutionary nation
with trade connections to the Soviet Union. Moscow gave Cuba
favorable conditions for trade with the interest of gaining the small
country's alliance in the Cold War. This new relationship brought
the threat of possible economic dependency to Cuba rather than
that of US-style imperialism.

January of 1959 brought Cuba a new beginning with many unknown possibilities. Castro visited the US in April at the invitation
of the Association of Newspaper Editors, and enthusiastic crowds
greeted him at every stop. At one point he met with Vice President
Richard Nixon, who asked him to comment on dictatorship and
democracy. Castro's response was, "Dictatorships are a shameful
blot on America, and democracy is more than just a word" (Franklin, 1997, p. 20). He went on to say that democracy is not compatible with hunger, unemployment, and injustice.

June of 1959 was when Che Guevara began three months of
global travel seeking support for Cuba's new government. He went
to developing nations such as Egypt, India, Indonesia, and Yugo-
slavia. He also visited Japan in search of new markets. His meeting
with the Soviet embassy in Cairo led to a Russian agreement to buy
Cuban sugar (Gott, 2004). Cuba had become a bastion for the cash
crop of sugar through colonialism and neocolonialism, and there
was no way to diversify its economy anytime soon. New markets for
sugar were necessary for the uncertain times ahead.

Not all governments of Latin America showed neutrality or
support for the Cuban Revolution. Cuba ended diplomatic relations with the Dominican Republic and its dictator, Leonidas Trujillo, in late June after learning of its Caribbean neighbor's plot to

overthrow the Cuban government. That plot was confirmed on August 10, when radio programming from the Dominican Republic urged Cubans to revolt against their government. Three days later the Cuban army captured ten occupants of a Dominican plane that had landed in central Cuba to distribute arms to counter-revolutionaries, and that ended the Dominican conspiracy (Escalante, 1995; Franklin, 1997).

Leftists and progressives from many countries viewed Cuba as a pioneer nation of youthful leadership with hope for new directions. Latin American writers who were emerging to become great novelists, such as Gabriel García Márquez and Carlos Fuentes, contributed to the cultural pages of *Revolución*, Cuba's newspaper of the Revolution (Gott, 2004). Editors of *Monthly Review*, an established socialist journal from the US, became fascinated with Cuba. Jean-Paul Sartre, considered the world's most famous philosopher at the time, visited Cuba in early 1960 and gave his enthusiastic approval for the Revolution.

As relations between the Cuban and US governments deteriorated, Cuba made new political and economic alliances. China followed the Soviet Union in July of 1960 in becoming a new importer of Cuban sugar. In the same month Soviet Premier Nikita Khrushchev promised to provide arms to Cuba in the event of a US invasion. The Organization of American States (OAS) met in Costa Rica on August 28 and adopted the US-sponsored Declaration of San José, which condemned any Soviet or Chinese attempt to engage in political or economic activity with Cuba or any American nation. The US government failed, though, to persuade the OAS to condemn the Cuban government. Cuban membership continued until the organization revoked it in 1962.

On September 2, 1960, Castro spoke to approximately a million Cubans in Revolution Plaza to confirm that the revolutionary ideas from *History will absolve me* had been implemented successfully. This speech became known as the First Declaration of Havana. The crowd had arrived to share in Castro's confidence that the Revolution was moving in the right direction. Castro denounced the Declaration of San José as well as the Monroe Doctrine. He also proclaimed Cuba's new direction in establishing trade relations with the Soviet Union and China while revealing Cuba's agreement to receive Soviet weapons. He affirmed the rights of all people to needs such as education, health care and jobs (Franklin, 1997; Gott, 2004).

Later that month Castro visited New York to address the UN general assembly. He became the first visiting president ever to stay in a hotel in Harlem. Enthusiastic crowds of black Harlem residents listened to Castro speak in the Hotel Theresa about the connections between US racist oppression at home and US imperialism abroad in Latin America. Among those visiting to hear Castro were Malcolm X, Langston Hughes, Soviet Premier Khrushchev, President Gamal Abdel Nasser of the United Arab Republic (Egypt and Syria), and Prime Minister Jawaharlal Nehru of India (Franklin, 1997; Gott, 2004).

The US government became increasingly alarmed at what it saw as Cuba's drift toward communism. Without the Platt Amendment as a means to occupy Cuba militarily, the US had turned to the weapon of economic sanctions. The Cold War front that had destroyed the democratic government of Arbenz in Guatemala was returning to Latin America with Cuba as the new target. As US anti-communist discourse grew toward Cuba in the Kennedy and Nixon campaigns, anti-imperialist discourse toward the US became more open in the government and the general population of Cuba.

Although Fidel Castro would not declare the socialist nature of the Cuban Revolution until April of 1961, he clearly was influenced in that direction long before that by two of his most trusted advisors—Che Guevara and Fidel's brother Raúl Castro (Farber, 1976). Both Guevara and Raúl Castro had been involved with the international communist movement. Raúl had travelled with a student delegation to Prague for a communist "peace congress" in June of 1953 as a representative of Cuba's Partido Socialista Popular. Guevara had been associated with leftist movements throughout Latin America and had developed an advanced knowledge of and affinity for Marxist theory while remaining independent from Marxist parties. Although neither of these two men was as charismatic as Fidel Castro, both played a large role in forming strategies to keep communist and non-communist sectors of Cuban society united during the initial stages of the post-triumphant Revolution.

Preparations for the Year of Education

The project of changing education in Cuba was not limited to the efforts of the Ministry of Education. A social movement was growing to build education reforms upon Law 680. Many of Cuba's prominent artists, including the poet Nicolás Guillén and the novelist Alejo Carpentier, dedicated their talents to support the Revolution and its plans for education. Haydée Santamaría Cuadrado, a female participant of the Moncada uprising, directed Casa de las Américas, an organization that promoted cultural awareness and civic education. The nation celebrated in August when 400 youth graduated to become the First Contingent of Volunteer Teachers for placement in rural areas. This growing movement was a legacy to the educational advances of the *Mambises* and the Rebel Army. Its core ideology of Cuban sovereignty and emancipation gained substance from the anti-imperialist and nationalist writings of Martí. It declared that literacy and quality education were human rights to be shared by all Cubans in the struggle to end the era of imperialism.

The elimination of illiteracy, along with transforming universities, was the first great challenge in the project for creating a new hegemony of education. The Revolutionary Armed Forces had established its program for fighting illiteracy and promoting a new civics education with help from the periodical *Arma Nueva* [new weapon]. The National Commission on Literacy and Fundamental Education (NCAEF) published the first record of civilian literacy work in September 1959. It gave numbers of literacy centers, students, and instructors in each of the six provinces and reported a national total of 844 centers serving 19,075 students with 2,832 instructors (Pérez Cruz, 2001). Within a year the Revolutionary Government was taking important steps to organize the mass movement that would become the National Literacy Campaign.

The two documents that became the textbooks for the Literacy Campaign were *Alfabeticemos* [Let's Teach Literacy] (Comisión Na-

cional de Alfabetización, 1961a) and *¡Venceremos!* [We will triumph!]
(Comisión Nacional de Alfabetización, 1961b). *Alfabeticemos* gave the
literacy instructors basic political content of the Revolution and a
set of guidelines on what and how to teach. It introduced 24 themes
of the Revolution and provided a glossary. *¡Venceremos!* was the
primer that instructors used while teaching. Meetings for creating
¡Venceremos!, beginning in February 1960, involved a collaboration
of the National College of Teacher Trainers, the NCAEF, and the
Ministry of Revolutionary Armed Forces. They set out to design a
primer that addressed the economic, social, and political needs of
the nation. Matilde Serra Robledo was a lead author of the primer
who later became a distinguished professor of pedagogy. She studied and applied "the pedagogical bibliography of the era, distinct
methods, and primers in use, which led to the selection of the
Global Sentence Method to give the student the necessary civic capacity, combined with the Syllabic Method for becoming literate"
(Comisión Nacional de Alfabetización y Educación Fundamental,
1961, p. 5, my translation). Some Latin American countries had
been using the Syllabic Method for decades. Although Paulo Freire
had used it in Brazil, he had no direct influence on Cuba's National
Literacy Campaign. Cuban educators applied a working draft of
¡Venceremos! to a pilot program for the first time on August 22, 1960.

On September 26, Fidel Castro spoke in New York before
delegates to the United Nations and made the following promise:
"In the coming year, our people intend to fight the great battle of
illiteracy, with the ambitious goal of teaching every single inhabi-
tant of the country to read and write in one year…" (as cited in
Kozol, 1978, p. 342). The Cuban government declared that the
coming year, 1961, would be the "Year of Education." The National Literacy Commission (CNA, shortened from the former
CNAEF) directed its Publicity Section to recruit literacy teachers
and to convince illiterate people of the need to become readers and
writers. Notices appeared in newspapers, magazines, and on posters, often with quotes by José Martí. The messages connected participation in the Literacy Campaign with civic dignity and revolutionary courage.

Castro's announcement of the forthcoming campaign before the UN likely troubled the US regarding Cuba's image throughout the Third World. If this kind of commitment to the education of all citizens were to be associated with leftist revolutions, then the US government's global appeal in the Cold War could be undermined. While the US remained caught in images of violent police force against growing struggles of the Civil Rights Movement, Cuba was moving forward to bring equal educational opportunity to all of its citizens regardless of ethnic or class background. The US had immense material wealth and military might, but Cuba had the idea of education as a human right for all. The possibility that other economically distressed nations could follow Cuba's lead in a revolution for education and in education for revolution presented a challenge to US hegemony in Latin America. Cuba was developing its own critical global citizenship in its bold nationalism and internationalism. How would the rest of Latin America respond? How would the US government respond?

4. Critical Global Citizenship in the Year of Education

I had never been aware of Cuba's National Literacy Campaign of 1961 until I visited Cuba for the first time at the end of 2001 as a graduate student. It was a winter-break course at the University of St. Thomas in Minneapolis that offered an introduction to education in Cuba with an 11-day visit to Havana. The itinerary included a morning at the Museum of the National Literacy Campaign. There we heard testimonies of a man and a woman who volunteered as teachers in the Campaign when they were teenagers. I left that morning wanting to learn more about this great national mobilization for literacy, and I ended up returning to Cuba the next two summers to conduct a literature review and to gather data for a dissertation.

A few articles and chapters about Cuba's National Literacy Campaign of 1961 have been published in English, and I am devoting two chapters to it here. In this chapter I will give a chronological account of the entire year of 1961, which the Cuban government called the Year of Education. In the next chapter I will discuss themes that emerged from testimonies I gathered of about 100 Cubans who participated in the 1961 Campaign. Both chapters will emphasize the themes of nationalism and internationalism in the context of critical global citizenship.

US ends diplomatic relations with Cuba

On January 3, 1961, President Eisenhower closed the US embassy in Havana and severed diplomatic relations. The two countries had seen their relations deteriorate since Cuba began nationalizing sugar and other industries dominated by US capital in the middle of 1959. This final step of closing the embassy revealed that the US government regarded Cuba as a serious enemy in the Cold War. A clandestine preparation for the Bay of Pigs invasion was underway, and Kennedy was no less hawkish than Eisenhower regarding the rebellious nation only 90 miles from Florida.

An early martyr

The Campaign was in a pilot stage when, on January 5, counter-revolutionaries assassinated an 18-year-old volunteer teacher in the mountainous Escambray region of the present-day province of Sancti Spíritus. The murderers left a note that included the words "of the profession of communist teacher." Castro (1961) declared in a public speech that "agents of imperialism…with yankee weapons" murdered Benítez because "he was young, he was black, he was a teacher, he was poor, and he was a worker (pp. 33-34)". Castro stated that Benítez would continue to be a teacher in that his violent death would inspire rather than deter others.

The Cuban journal for emerging readers titled *Arma Nueva* [New Weapon] featured a sketch of Benítez on the cover of its January-to-March issue with the words "Maestro y Martir" [Teacher and Martyr] (Comisión Nacional de Alfabetización, 1961c). The same issue featured a photograph of a somber crowd of Cuban youth holding up posters with the drawn image of Benítez's face. It also included a poem by an author identified as "El Indio Naborí" in tribute to the young martyr. Topics among the brief articles appearing in the same issue were US-occupied Guantánamo Bay, decolonization in Africa, nationalization of Cuban industries, and a feature on agricultural cooperatives near the town of Los Pinos in the province of Pinar del Rio.

Before long, all literacy instructors who left their homes to teach in rural zones became known as Conrado Benítez *brigadistas*. The image of Benítez appeared on posters for recruiting young volunteers to teach. The booklet of revolutionary themes titled *Cumpliremos* [We will finish], read by all teaching recruits who would leave their homes, included on its cover a shield symbol with the images of a pencil and an open book showing the letter "a" for *alfabetización* [literacy] and with the words *Ejercito de Alfabetizadores – Brigadas Conrado Benítez* [Army of Literacy Teachers – Conrado Benítez Brigades] (Comisión Nacional de Alfabetización, 1961d).

Organizing a mass movement

Many teachers had left Cuba for the US out of opposition to the Revolution. Cuba's illiteracy rate stood at 23.6 percent of the Cuban population age 10 and above in the most recent census of 1953, and the task of eliminating illiteracy would require a massive collaboration between the government and civil society. The National Literacy Commission, operating within the Ministry of Education, designated the months of January to April as the period of creating an organizational and technical structure for the Campaign. The full implementation of the instructional work was scheduled for May.

The National Literacy Commission consisted of four departments—Technical, Publicity, Finance, and Publication (Lorenzetto & Neys, 1965). The Technical Department managed the logistics for organizing the mass movement. It organized the teaching and non-teaching personnel needed for making the Campaign possible. The Publicity Department recruited volunteers to teach and urged illiterate people to accept instruction. The Finance Department took care of managing revenues and expenses. The Publication Department printed the manual, primer, and other documents used in the Campaign. Eighteen Integrated Revolutionary Organizations (ORIs) committed their resources to the work of one or more of these departments.

The Technical Department made it possible for the majority of Cubans to contribute in various ways to the efforts of the Campaign. It ensured that all volunteer instructors received pedagogical support from at least one professional educator. Organizations such as the National Federation of Private Schools and the National School of Teachers gave their support. In order to bring young instructors to the most remote rural areas, bridges needed to be built, roads and trails needed improvements, and truck drivers needed to be hired. These efforts received support from ORIs such as the Confederation of Cuban Workers and the Federation of Rural Worker Associations.

The Publicity Department did the work of persuading people to participate in the Campaign. I spent a couple hours one day in the

Museum of the National Literacy Campaign viewing volumes of advertisements that had appeared on posters and in journals. The ads began appearing in October of 1960, and in early 1961 they were everywhere in Cuba. Many used famous quotes by Martí. One such quote that appeared often was this: "Knowing how to read is knowing how to walk. Knowing how to write is knowing how to fly (my translation)." What followed this was the charge, "If you know, teach; if you don't know, learn." The ads often appealed to Cubans' sense of revolutionary nationalism. One poster advertising literacy classes in local schools ended with this: "We will win the war against illiteracy like we won the war for our political and economic independence." Many artists contributed to the designs of posters. Programs and ads from the radio added to the cause as well. The Independent Front of Free Broadcasters and the National Association of Advertisers, as ORIs, contributed their resources. Also, the Federation of Cuban Women, another ORI, recruited women as teachers and students in the Campaign. Before the triumph of the Revolution, there were many maids and prostitutes who were illiterate. The new expectation was that maids would become organized as advocates for their own interests and that prostitution would become extinct.

The Campaign came with many costs, and the Finance Department of the National Literacy Commission worked to secure funds and to manage the budget. Calculating the financial cost of the Campaign was difficult because the *brigadistas* contributed to their own needs to a great extent with their work by day in the agricultural cooperatives. By night they taught with lanterns that the Chinese government provided at minimal cost. A final post-Campaign estimate placed the government's spending at 20 million pesos, but that is only a fraction of an unquantifiable total including the immense material and financial contributions from Campaign participants, workers in solidarity, and mass organizations of civil society. This collaboration between state and civil society amounted to a mass solidarity behind the revolutionary literacy project. In an interview with Jonathan Kozol (1978), Raúl Ferrer, national vice-coordinator of the Campaign, stated

The treasure of the Third World is the treasure of our people, not their cash. We do not deny the necessity of money; but, in these kinds of struggles, the real price is something which cannot be put in numbers. (p. 372)

This quote indicates the internationalism and critical global citizenship that Cuban leaders embraced. Ferrer focused on all people of the Third World and not only on Cubans.

Finally, the Campaign needed published texts, and the Publication Department of the National Literacy Commission printed them. The manual *Alfabeticemos* and the primer *¡Venceremos!* [We will triumph!] were the central texts of the Campaign. The booklet *Cumpliremos* [We will finish] gave the *brigadistas* further readings on the themes of the Revolution and the importance of their work. The Publication Department collaborated with the Publicity Department to produce mass printings of advertisements for the Campaign.

Content of the Campaign publications

The three publications worked together not only as tools for literacy instruction but also as civics textbooks for the Revolution. Themes of nationalism and internationalism together supported the growing idea of a critical global citizenship. The texts presented Cuba as a truly independent nation for the first time as a result of the Revolution's triumph. They named counter-revolutionary forces in the US and Cuba as the enemy. They also emphasized that solidarity with the Revolution came from citizens of nations around the world, including the US.

The first text that volunteer instructors studied was the 98-page manual *Alfabeticemos* (Comisión Nacional de Alfabetización, 1961a). It begins with a poem (anonymous) followed by a quote from Martí: "…And I became a teacher, which means I became a creator (p. 4, my translation)." An introduction addressed to the instructors emphasizes that the Campaign would be a labor of all the Cuban people. It describes illiteracy as the "product of underdevelopment provoked by the intervention of imperialism and indirect product of the backward political economy of the nation" (p. 5). It went on to say that illiteracy is a powerful enemy that must and will be defeated.

The first part of *Alfabeticemos* is titled "Orientations for the Literacy Instructor." The first of three sub-sections provides guidance for establishing trust with students of all ages. It tells instructors to show interest in the students' problems, to help them understand why the present was the best time to have a national literacy campaign, to remember that many students would have physical or social conditions that could bring challenges to learning, and to establish a schedule for daily lessons of about two hours. The second sub-section explains how to use the primer *¡Venceremos!* with its 13 lessons. Examples of what to say when starting different parts of a lesson are followed by general guidelines for delivering instruction. The final subsection addresses observations concerning the teaching of certain rules for pronouncing vowels and syllables.

The second and lengthiest part of *Alfabeticemos* is titled "Themes of Revolutionary Orientation." It introduces 24 themes, many of which are addressed directly in the content of *¡Venceremos!*. Each theme begins with a quote, and nearly every one is from Castro or Martí. The first theme, with the subheading "The Revolution," explains that an armed revolution was necessary to defeat foreign domination and to establish a new order for "liberty, work, land, school, and respect for whoever struggles and works (p. 23)". Some of the other themes that address Cuban nationalism within internationalism are "Friends and Enemies," "Imperialism," "International Trade," "War and Peace," and "International Unity." "Literacy" is the 22nd theme, and the final two are "The Revolution wins all battles" and "The Declaration of Havana."

The third and final part of the manual is a 20-page glossary titled "Vocabulary." Many of the featured words and phrases pertain to internationalism in the senses of resistance against foreign domination and of cultivating alliances. Some examples are *antiimperialista, bloqueo económico* [economic blockade], *Brigadas Internacionales de Trabajo* [International Brigades of Workers], *capitales extranjeros* [foreign capital], *colonialismo, comercio internacional, Doctrina de Monroe, Enmienda Platt* [Platt Amendment], *EUA* [USA], *explotación* [exploitation], *Federación Sindical Mundial* [World Federation of Unions], *guerras justas* [just wars], *Hatuey* (Taíno rebel leader against Spanish conquest), *independencia, Latinoamericanismo* (Latin American unity against imperialism), *monopolios extranjeros* [foreign monopolies], *Nikita Jruchov* (Soviet prime minister Krushchev), *OEA* [Organization of American States], *ONU* [United Nations], *paz mundial* [world peace], *población indígena* [indigenous population], *países semicoloniales* [semi-colonized nations], *países socialistas* [socialist nations], *países subdesarrollados* [underdeveloped nations], *Reforma Arancelaria* (Cuban law that charges tariffs), *rescatar las riquezas del país* [recovering national riches from foreigners], *Roa* (last name of Cuba's Minister of Foreign Relations), *soberanía* [sovereignty], *Soviet, unidad internacional* [international unity], *URSS* [USSR], and *yanqui*. *AP* and *UPI* are presented as US news agencies serving the interests of "yankee imperialism." Education in the Cuban Revolution clearly was forging a new critical global citizenship with a bold anti-imperialist hegemony.

¡Venceremos! served as the primer or textbook for literacy instruction in the Campaign (Comisión Nacional de Alfabetización, 1961b). It provided 13 lessons that brought the students to a first-grade level of literacy. It used the syllabic method (photographs to syllables to words to sentences) that had been used in literacy drives in other countries, but a major difference was that Cuba's Campaign used political themes in the content that resonated with the experiences of the students. Some lessons provided themes of internationalism.

The first lesson begins with a photograph of a meeting of the Organization of American States (OAS), which has the Spanish acronym OEA. This provides a pretext for learning the letters that represent three of the five vowel sounds in Spanish. The OAS also happens to be the international organization that made it possible for foreign capital, primarily from the US, to dominate land holdings in Cuba. The rural families that were left landless by OAS policy were often left without education and basic literacy as well. This first lesson engaged students in learning because it started with their experience. The lessons that followed gave the Revolution's nationalist and egalitarian solutions in agriculture, homeownership, public health, recreation, militias, and industry.

The final lesson in ¡*Venceremos!* returns to internationalism with the subheading "Cuba is not alone." The photograph shows a crowd with a banner reading "Solidaridad con Cuba" [Solidarity with Cuba]. The banner also shows the Cuban flag blended in with what appears to be a flag of another nation with three horizontal stripes (black and white photo). A short paragraph follows: "People of all nations help us. United we will defeat the aggression. They cannot stop the Revolution. Shouts of liberty come from people of all nations."

A third publication for use by *brigadistas* was *Cumpliremos* (Comisión Nacional de Alfabetización, 1961d). This book of 141 pages expanded upon themes introduced in *Alfabeticemos*. The introduction, addressed to "Young literacy instructor," places Cuban illiteracy and the Revolution in political, economic, and social contexts. It includes a passage that refutes the idea that Cuba was becoming a satellite of the Soviet Union and China, claiming that this was a lie perpetrated by the US media. The first chapter, without a title, focuses on Cuba's history as a 'semi-colony' under the US from 1902 to 1958. Some chapter titles that follow show a direct inclusion of Cuba's changing international relations: "The Revolution defeated imperialism," "Nationalization of corporations," "Differences between the heroism of the revolutionary and the crime of the counter-revolutionary," and "Revolutionaries and counter-revolutionaries." These last two, being the final of ten chapters, explain how Cuba by necessity became a trade partner with socialist nations after the US government imposed the economic blockade. They also contrast trade relations with capitalist and socialist nations, the latter not coming from the objective of exploitation. The final chapter names US imperialism as the greatest enemy of the Cuban Revolution and ends with a passionate call for an end to exploitation in Cuba.

The three documents together gave the young *brigadistas* the tools for combating not only illiteracy but also the ideology that kept so many Cubans oppressed without land and education. Cuba was undergoing revolutionary change, and the government entrusted adolescents to play a major part in the transformation. These youth, who had been too young to fight in the Revolutionary

War, were becoming the soldiers for the war against illiteracy. Their schools were cancelled to make the Campaign possible, but they were to learn lessons that could never be learned with books alone and within school walls.

Popular literacy teachers

It was not only rural areas that had illiterate people. Urban neighborhoods also had residents of all ages who could neither read nor write. For these people the Campaign needed volunteer instructors who lived nearby. Such instructors became known as *alfabetizadores populares* [popular literacy teachers]. The popular literacy teachers were of a broader age range than the *Conrado Benítez brigadistas*. Some eager adolescents and pre-adolescents did not receive parental permission to live and teach in rural zones, and many of these youth became popular literacy teachers in their own urban neighborhoods.

The popular literacy teachers contributed to the Campaign part-time in varying degrees. Some had enough time to work with only a single student, and others taught more than one family. Some taught for a few weeks, and others for the entire Campaign. Unlike the Conrado Benítez *brigadistas*, these instructors already knew the territory where they would teach and likely knew their students beforehand. They did not receive mass training as the *brigadistas* did, but they underwent training and ongoing coaching by professional teachers as well.

Training of Conrado Benítez brigadistas

The Conrado Benítez *brigadistas* had an average age of fifteen. Before embarking on a journey to a remote rural region to teach literacy, these mostly urban youth needed orientation and training. The seven-day training began with a first cohort in mid-April and continued with others through the end of August. The place was a resort at Cuba's beautiful Varadero Beach, which before the Revolution had been a favorite spot for affluent vacationers from the US and Cuba. The young trainees learned how to use *¡Alfabeticemos!* and

Venceremos, and they attended classes on revolutionary politics, personal conduct, and rural public health. They also had time for sports, the beach, and movies (Fagen, 1969).

The government wanted to minimize risks to the health of the *brigadistas* and provided them with a medical examination and vaccinations before they went to their assigned posts (Ordóñez Careller, 1995). The government also gave the instructors information on the prevention of diseases that were common in rural areas. The *brigadistas* later shared this information with their hosts in an effort to increase awareness of the diseases and their prevention.

The first cohort at Varadero arrived the day before the Bay of Pigs invasion. There were about a thousand girls and a thousand boys. During May, the training center expanded to a capacity for 7,500 trainees. More than 200 teachers provided lessons in physical education, politics, and instructional strategies. Other teachers, after receiving training, went with the young instructors to the countryside. The trainers worked to instill a revolutionary sense of purpose in the *brigadistas*. The youth were reminded often that they were playing a central role in making Cuban history. When the program ended in August, about 105,700 instructors had completed the training (Fagen, 1969).

Campaign interrupted

The Bay of Pigs invasion came right as the Campaign was underway as a mass mobilization. The invaders, mostly Cubans who had left for the US upon the Revolution's triumph, flew from Nicaragua and conducted aerial bombings of Cuban air bases on the 15th of April. Two days later, the attack on Playa Girón (Bay of Pigs) began. Reinforcements on the 18th included six US pilots flying three bombers, and four of them were killed (Franklin, 1997). When one of the bodies was recovered, Cubans had evidence of direct US involvement. The Revolutionary Armed Forces defeated the invasion within days, and the Literacy Campaign continued despite the constant threat from counter-revolutionary bands.

Castro declared the socialist nature of the Revolution on April 16, when Cubans were reeling from the aerial attacks of the previous day that killed seven people. The Cuban people could have reacted with a wary anti-communism. Instead, they claimed socialism as their own with roots in Martí's anti-imperialism. From then on, the political content of the Campaign included discussion of Cuba's new openly socialist direction, but the inspirational heroes of the Campaign continued to be Martí and Castro, much more so than Marx, Engels, and Lenin.

A mass mobilization

The defeat of the Bay of Pigs invasion left Cubans with an emboldened sense of anti-imperialism in the Revolution and its Literacy Campaign. Castro announced on May 1 that all private schools would be nationalized. Secondary schools, as planned since January, closed in April to enable students and teachers to contribute full-time to the Campaign. Youth continued to become *brigadistas* with parental consent. The numbers of popular literacy teachers also continued to grow. Municipal Councils of Education increased their efforts to identify all illiterate adults in their vicinity and to persuade them to become literate.

The Campaign at the local level was organized carefully. The Municipal Literacy Council oversaw neighborhood commissions, which in turn supervised literacy units. Each literacy unit by design had a leader who coordinated efforts among one licensed teacher, 25 literacy instructors, and 50 illiterate people. The licensed teacher, known as the *asesor técnico* [technical assessor], served as consultant and coach to the 25 instructors. Having two students per instructor was the goal, but that was not always possible.

Behind the scenes countless contributions continued from ORIs, but another source of grassroots organizing came from the Committees for Defense of the Revolution (CDRs). Castro announced the creation of CDRs in a public speech on September 28, 1960. They were to be units of vigilance against counterrevolutionary penetration at the block level of every neighborhood and small town. Following the Bay of Pigs invasion, the CDRs heightened their sense of urgency in guarding against potential attacks from enemies still living in Cuba. CDRs created an environment in which neighbors knew each other, and these organized units were instrumental in persuading illiterate neighbors to accept the Campaign's offer to bring reading and writing to their lives along with the political themes of the content.

Many illiterate people had eyesight too defective for reading. By the end of the Campaign, 177,000 people received eyeglasses at the government's expense (MacDonald, 1985). The facilities in Cuba that produced glasses normally had made 6,000 pairs in the same period. This increased production occurred despite the fact that a third of Cuba's opticians had fled after the Revolution's triumph.

The Campaign mobilized civil society and placed the family at the center (Pérez Cruz, 2001). A single Conrado Benítez *brigadista* or a single popular literacy teacher often worked with an entire family. In many cases the teacher and the family formed a bond that continued well beyond the end of the Campaign. Such bonds, in conjunction with the close ties within literacy units, created a foundation for unifying the nation within the Revolution.

The dynamics of relations between Conrado Benítez *brigadistas* and their students were a large part of the legend of the Campaign. Teacher and student typically had nothing in common other than a belief in the importance of the Campaign and the Revolution for Cuba, and even that bond was not always guaranteed. The *brigadista* typically was a 14- or 15-year-old middle-class urbanite, and the students were primarily adults living in rural poverty that had existed for many generations through colonial and neocolonial times. The youngest *brigadista* was eight, and the oldest student was a 106-year-old woman who was a former slave.

A typical day had the teacher working with the family on routine tasks. Female *brigadistas* often helped with cooking and taking care of children, while the males usually worked in the fields that grew sugar, coffee, or other crops. Each visiting teacher had a hammock supplied during training because the peasant families typically did not have an extra bed in their small dwellings. Female teachers were housed with designated host families, and male teachers lived with the families with whom they worked and taught. At night the instruction for literacy took place in the family's house at a table under the Chinese lantern. The *brigadistas* learned about the toils of working the land and about the poverty that rural families had experienced through the exploitation and neglect of colonialism and neocolonialism. The rural families learned how to read and write while receiving an introduction to the central tenets of the Cuban Revolution, including agrarian reform. Many of these families had members that had joined the Rebel Army to fight in the Revolutionary War, and now it was time for the youth of privileged urban families to sacrifice their comfort in service to the Revolution. The harsh conditions of life in the isolated rural zones took a toll, and 62 *brigadistas* died due to illnesses or accidents (Keeble, 2001).

In addition to breaking the urban-rural divide in Cuba, the Campaign went far in destroying old barriers of racism and sexism. There were many Conrado Benítez *brigadistas* of African descent. Some taught in zones where white families at first resisted the prospect of having a black teacher. Many of these same families later would regard their young black teachers as if they had become beloved family members. The majority of the *brigadistas* were female, and some rural families doubted that an adolescent girl or young woman from the city could handle harsh rural conditions. These female teachers became like sisters and daughters to many families after gaining the respect of their hosts and students.

On July 6, the Council of Ministers of the Revolutionary Government enacted the Education Nationalization Law. This abolished private schooling and declared that all teaching institutions would promote proletarian interests. It served to unite the nation in what Ferrer (1961) called a "new culture and moral conscience" (p. 62). Education became a source of egalitarian ethics and would no longer be a system of class privilege.

Between July and August the census workers increased efforts to locate illiterate people and to persuade them to accept instruction, and the number identified in that period increased from 735,426 to 985,322 (Comisión Nacional de Alfabetización, as cited by Pérez Cruz, 2001). Municipal Councils of Education worked with CDRs and ORIs to get a figure as accurate as possible of the numbers of illiterate people. They wanted everyone to know that there was no shame in being illiterate in 1961 but that to be illiterate in 1962 would be a missed opportunity to participate fully in Cuba's changing society.

From September 2 to 4, national, provincial and local leaders of the Campaign met in Havana for the Second Congress of Municipal Councils of Education and determined that the Campaign was not on pace for finishing successfully by December. Armando Hart addressed the convention with the historical significance of the Campaign: "Never have the teachers and students of the people of Latin America had the opportunity of this nature in which they identify more each day with the people, toward the attainment of their ideals" (Congreso Nacional de Alfabetización, 1961e, p. 9, my translation). During the convention, Raúl Ferrer coined the term "QTATA², " which in Spanish sounds like "koo-tata al cuadrado [*al cuadrado* meaning 'squared']." This acronym meant "*Que todo analfabeto tenga alfabetizador, que todo alfabetizador tenga analfabeto*" [That every illiterate person has a literacy teacher, that every literacy teacher has an illiterate person]. This phrase was ubiquitous in radio announcements targeting illiterate people either not yet identified or not yet committed to instruction. These same announcements, in addition to posters, reached out also to potential instructors who had not yet decided to teach.

The Second Congress heard testimonies of delegates from other countries in Latin America. Expressions of solidarity came from these visitors from Venezuela, Colombia, and Brazil. Ricardo Santana, a Colombian professor and journalist, spoke of what Cuba's Revolution meant for so many in Latin America: "Cuba has become a vanguard, the vanguard most conscious and lucid of our America" (Congreso Nacional de Alfabetización, 1961e, p. 74, my translation). All three international speakers conveyed a hope that their countries would follow Cuba's example in defying imperialism and embracing a nationalist revolution with the political will to educate all citizens. The Report of the International Commission to the Second Congress addressed the grave problem of illiteracy in many parts of the world and how socialist nations were taking great measures to eradicate it.

Intensified efforts

The Campaign needed many more instructors to meet the needs of the expanded number of illiterate people identified. The solution became the recruitment of literate workers. These new teaching forces were called *brigadas Patria o Muerte* [Homeland or Death brigades]. These workers continued to receive their regular pay, and their co-workers who stayed behind worked extra hours to make up for the lost production. Most of the *Patria o Muerte* instructors went to live and teach in rural zones with the greatest need, but many taught their illiterate co-workers in their own workplaces. Census workers had identified 50,000 illiterate workers in 3,442 work sites. In September, the labor unions reported that 36,019 workers were studying to become readers and writers. As of August 30, approximately 30,000 *Patria o Muerte* instructors were enlisted for teaching, and about half of these continued teaching through the end of the Campaign in December (Fagen, 1969; Pérez Cruz, 2001).

On September 18, participation in the Campaign by professional teachers became mandatory. A "plan of attendance" employed volunteers, including parents and the Association of Young Rebels, to keep children occupied with educational activities while their teachers were busy as technical assessors in the Campaign. Out of a total of 36,000 professional teachers in Cuba, 34,700 participated in the Campaign (Fagen, 1969; Pérez Cruz, 2001).

On November 5, Melena del Sur became the first municipality to declare itself free of illiteracy, and Hart and Castro spoke at the celebration there. Other towns followed throughout November and December with their announcements and celebrations. "Acceleration camps" appeared wherever a significant number of adults were struggling with the lessons. Municipalities entered a friendly competition to finish their work and employed a process of "emulation" in which successful practices in one zone were shared freely with others. Every Municipal Literacy Council wanted to finish the mission in time to join in a national celebration before Christmas.

Tragically, another young teacher became a murder victim on November 26. According to Castro's account, counter-revolutionary bands led Manuel Ascunce, age 16, and the father of his host family, Pedro Lantigua, at gunpoint to a tree and hanged them (Fagen, 1969). Like Conrado Benítez, Ascunce became a martyr who inspired Cubans to finish the work of the Campaign. Castro in a speech declared that the assassins wanted the Cuban people to give up on the Campaign out of fear but that solidarity with Ascunce's family would not allow that to happen. Other leaders spoke of the people avenging Ascunce's death by strengthening commitments to end the Campaign successfully.

Completing and celebrating

At the end of the Campaign each newly literate student wrote a letter to Castro, and I reviewed 102 of those letters, 17 from each of the six provinces, in the Museum of the Literacy Campaign. These letters included 23 favorable and enthusiastic references to 'socialism' and none that were unfavorable. The two words that were included in just about every letter were "thanks" and "revolution."

Municipalities continued to declare that they were free of illiteracy, and efforts were intensified in remaining zones to reach the same point. When their work was finished, many Conrado Benítez *brigadistas* and their host families had a bittersweet separation after working and living together for months. Trains and buses took the young teachers to Havana for the final celebration to be held on December 22, which would leave time for them to be home for Christmas.

The celebration was a grand event held in the Plaza of the Revolution next to the large statue of José Martí and the tall monument built in his honor. A total of 308,000 instructors had contributed their work, and many were present (Fagen, 1969). Conrado Benítez *brigadistas* were in uniform as they marched to the plaza. Some held flags reading "*¡Vencimos!*" [We conquered] with the emblem for Conrado Benítez *brigadistas*, and others carried a Cuban flag and giant pencils (Keeble, 2001).

There was much to celebrate at the Campaign's end. Only 272,000 Cubans remained illiterate, which was 3.9 percent of the nation's population. This gave Cuba the highest literacy rate among all nations in Latin America. It was a mass movement that received the participation of a large proportion of the population. Out of a total of 7 million Cubans, 1.25 million participated either as an instructor or a student. Two million Cubans were too young to participate, which meant that one in four eligible people participated directly (Fagen, 1969).

In my reflection on the Campaign I now will turn to three themes. First, the accomplishments by adolescents and even pre-adolescents as instructors demonstrates that young people can play an important role in the transformation of a society. Second, the Campaign was a mass movement of popular education in addition to being a state-supported project. Third, international solidarity with the Campaign, including direct participation by some foreigners as instructors, was a source of strength that countered the efforts of the US government to undermine the Revolution. All three of these themes contribute to my broader focus on critical global citizenship.

Civic engagement of youth

When young people feel alienated, they can become cynical. When they feel valued, they can become inspired. The Cuban Revolution valued young people by immediately and intentionally revolutionizing education. Military posts became school buildings, and education became a human right rather than a privilege of elites. When the Cuban government made the commitment to eradicate illiteracy in one year, the only way possible was to employ school-age volunteers as instructors. Hart and other educational leaders had faith that young people, with parental consent, would be willing and able to complete the task.

When in US history have adolescents received trust to complete a mission that can compare? Of course, the US has experienced glorious movements for ending slavery, for gaining women's suffrage, and for ending legal racial segregation. How were youth involved in these movements? One example that comes to mind is when most of the African American adults in Birmingham had been jailed for expressing rage at Jim Crow segregation, and then their children continued their demonstrations until police arrested them, too. Youth everywhere have the capacity to recognize injustice and to act in correcting it.

Since the ideology of Manifest Destiny took hold early in its history, the US has developed a chauvinist nationalism, quite different from the emancipatory nationalism that propelled the Cuban Revolution. "Serving one's country" in the US has become synonymous with volunteering in the military. Slogans such as "protecting our freedom" have taken on a life of their own while pushing out any space for critical inquiry into the root causes of US wars. Civics is a one-semester course in high school where students typically cram their short-term memories for tests and then put it all to rest. Courses in US and world history follow the same pattern. The secondary schools of the entire nation use textbooks in social studies that celebrate a few heroes of movements without focusing on the grassroots struggles of ordinary people who made movements possible. Students learn that they must wait passively for the next hero to emerge when the need arises. Young people feel alienated when they are bombarded with advertisements telling them what to buy next in order to feel like a complete human being. As Jean Anyon's (1980) research has shown, schools train the working- and middle-class youth to become obedient workers and middle managers, respectively, and they educate the few elite to become leaders and, by virtue of their class privilege, defenders of the status quo.

US educators can, and some do, imagine and embrace a different paradigm. Critical educators understand that knowledge is power and that students construct knowledge either for their empowerment or for cynicism. Such teachers choose to foster change agency in students in order that they can become active citizens in a society that can move closer to a participatory democracy. Students fortunate enough to experience this kind of education have opportunities to question policies and policymakers in their schools, communities, nation, and world. Their questioning then can lead to critical reflection and collective action to correct injustices. Their concept of democracy can grow beyond the idea of mere voting to include the well-being of all citizens through education and health care as human rights.

Most critical educators in the US likely are political progressives who would not identify themselves as revolutionaries in deep solidarity with the Cuban Revolution. However, if they were to understand the tremendous accomplishments of youth in the Cuban National Literacy Campaign, then they would better understand the potential in youth to play a large role in a project that transforms a society. Granted, the US almost certainly will not experience a revolution anytime soon that resembles the Cuban Revolution, but every critical educator in the US can act on the faith that students are fully capable of becoming global citizens with the power to create a society and a world that are more just and humane.

Popular education

Education is a part of culture that cannot exist outside of politics. When a small group of elites in a society has a disproportionately large share of power, they organize to protect their interest in the status quo. They use their power and wealth to influence school boards, state and national educational policymakers, and textbook companies. The public schools, as such, become institutions of socialization where students learn to fit into society as it is. It then becomes necessary for progressives to form their own educational projects. These formal or informal projects often are identified as examples of "popular education."

Popular education has its historic roots in the French Revolution, but Paulo Freire is the best known proponent in recent decades (Kerka, 1997). It generally is associated with community-based adult education for progressive social change. Early examples in the US are in the labor movement of the 1920s and 30s and the Highlander Folk School of Tennessee with its organizing campaigns for labor struggles and the Civil Rights Movement. In Latin America as well there were manifestations of popular education in labor movements of the 1920s and 30s, with Cuba's Julio Antonio Mella and student-worker educational coalitions as an example.

The phrase "popular education" was not used during Cuba's National Literacy Campaign, nor was it used commonly anywhere at that time even though the concept had been put into practice during numerous social movements around the world. Barbara Smith (2008), whose dissertation is a case study on popular education in Cuba, stated it well in regard to the Campaign: "If we consider popular education to be an education by the people and for the people, then the Cuban Literacy Campaign of 1961 was one of the largest popular education programs ever undertaken" (p. 24).

The Campaign was not an example of popular education in the traditional sense. It was not in opposition to a reactionary or conservative government, nor was it trying to push the envelope with a liberal government. Instead, it was in compliance with a revolutionary government. In a global sense, though, it was popular education in opposition to neocolonialism under the political, economic and social hegemony of the US. The US government and US corporations in Cuba never had the political will to eradicate illiteracy in Cuba during the neocolonial era. On the contrary, they knew that a population with universal access to literacy and formal education is harder to exploit. The Campaign became the beginning of Cuba's popular education against foreign domination and for national sovereignty, against economic exploitation and for an egalitarian political economy.

Critical global education

I already have highlighted the aspects of internationalism in the content of didactic materials used in the Campaign. There not only was a resistance to US domination but also an effort to connect with struggles of the people throughout Latin America and all of the so-called Third World. The words of anti-imperialism from Martí and Castro are directed to all of Latin America when they speak of "Our America." The Campaign's legacy has stretched far beyond Cuba. An education for critical global citizenship is the greatest weapon against the extremism of what has become neoliberal capitalism, and the Campaign was a catalyst of this education in grand proportion.

International support for Cuba's Campaign was evident when delegates from three other Latin American countries spoke at the Second Congress of Municipal Councils of Education. Even more impressive was that foreigners became Conrado Benítez *brigadistas* in the Campaign. The Cuban newspaper *Revolución* paid tribute to these visitors from different Latin American countries in articles late in the year. Five instructors from Argentina (Murillo, Vigo, Torres, Romani & Beltran, 1964) later wrote about how their students in Cuba received them: "That five Argentine teachers went to Cuba overcoming the difficulties of persecution, having traveled more than 10,000 kilometers to be with them [Cubans] and struggle with them against ignorance, filled them with joy" (p. 62, my translation). When these Argentines arrived in Cuba, an Ecuadoran instructor told them that their wisdom would be in resembling the Cuban people, which the Argentine teachers took to mean in doing what the Cubans were doing. The Argentines wrote that for a very long time they would cherish their memories of the Cubans they taught.

Many of the Cubans whom I interviewed spoke passionately of their sense of global citizenship while remembering their work as instructors or students in the Campaign. At the time of the Campaign many of the instructors were too young to understand the full scale of what they would do for the Revolution, and most of the students had not developed a broad understanding of the world due to their illiterate condition. In reflection 42 years later, they knew that their accomplishments in Cuba opened the door to many possibilities around the world.

5. The Campaign from Testimonies of Participants

When people participate together in a project that changes the course of history, their memories need to be recorded. World War II veterans and survivors of the Nazi Holocaust are advancing in age, and their testimonies are being saved in books, films, and museums. The participants in Cuba's National Literacy Campaign do not have their experiences recorded in many media, especially outside of Cuba. The Conrado Benítez *brigadistas*, as of this writing, are approaching an average age of 65, and the vast majority of their students are quite a bit older. These ordinary heroes of the Cuban Revolution are not likely to be the subjects of media projects that receive large endowments from international capital. If their stories are to reach a wide global audience, more operators of alternative media need to take time to visit Cuba to gather the precious memories that so many Cubans have of their educational Revolution. This is a part of history that must not be a mere footnote regarding the development of critical global citizenship.

All of the testimonies of Campaign participants in this chapter are from personal communications that I had with people through interviews or focus groups during the summer of 2003. Nearly all interviews took place in the participants' homes, and focus groups met me wherever a conference room was available. Participants received no payment for their time; indeed, many laughed when they heard me say that participants in US educational research sometimes did. Quotations are from my translations of transcripts in Spanish. Around 100 people in different parts of Cuba volunteered their time to meet with me and tell their recollections of the Campaign. Among them were those who became literate, those who taught, those who supervised the instructors, and some who contributed to the nation's project in a variety of other ways. My Spanish was not super-fluent, and I relied on the bilingual expertise of my interpreter Julio Macías Macías, a former employee of the Cuban Embassy in Canada. Also, the Cuban member of my dissertation committee, Felipe de J. Pérez Cruz, took considerable time from his usual duties with the Centro de Estudios de América [Center of American Studies] to make arrangements for my interviews and focus groups in and outside of Havana. The scope and quality of my work would have been severely limited without their support. Also, I cannot forget the hospitality of Dolores Guerra and Luis Montes de Oca, friends of Felipe who provided room and board to me at a rate that was affordable in contrast to the tourist hotels, guest houses, and restaurants of Havana.

Alfabetizados: Students in the Campaign

Approximately 707,000 Cubans learned to read and write for the first time in 1961, and I feel fortunate to have been able to hear and record testimonies of several. In Spanish they are called *alfabetizados* [alphabetized]. They described their lives before the triumph of the Revolution and before the Campaign. They shared their memories of the triumph and how they felt then. They spoke of how they learned about the Campaign and how they decided to study. Some *alfabetizados* spoke to me in detail about the learning process that they experienced and about their instructors and fellow students. There also were words of how they felt about themselves at the end of the Campaign, how much they continued to study, and their current opinions of the Campaign, Cuba, and socialism. Finally, they responded to my questions concerning their views on citizenship and patriotism.

The first *alfabetizado* to meet with me was not a student during the Campaign but rather was a member of the Rebel Army who became literate during the Revolutionary War. Antonio Ovidio Naranjo García (personal communication, June 27, 2003) was in his early 20s when he fought in Fidel Castro's division in the Sierra Maestro Mountains of eastern Cuba. He had had a few lessons in reading then but still could not write his name. Regarding his relations with other soldiers who studied, he said, "There were 20 of us in the school, and we were all equal, like family, always helping each other." After the triumph of the Revolution, he was stationed in Havana. He went to fight against the Bay of Pigs invasion at Playa Girón, and a close friend of his died in battle. He continued his education to the 10th grade and became a construction leader in Havana.

Living in the same Havana neighborhood as Antonio was Candido Merencio Gamboa (personal communication, June 29, 2003), whom I met while he was decorating his house for the 50th anniversary celebration of the attack on the Moncada barracks. The son of illiterate *campesinos* in Guantánamo, he became literate in the Campaign at age sixteen. He told me how his childhood education was cut short: "My father was a peasant and the owner of a small piece of land; and at the age that I was able to work the farm with him, I went to work." His father and older brothers had fought against Batista's army. Candido had one teacher in the Campaign—a 25-year-old woman who taught many people. After the Campaign, he continued his studies through the 6th grade while in the army. He went on to become a construction worker in Havana.

I did not have the opportunity to interview other *alfabetizados* of the Campaign until weeks later when I visited an area known as La Cienaga—the location of the Bay of Pigs invasion. In the bayside town of Playa Larga I met with Teresa Fernandez Miranda (personal communication, August 1, 2003), a mulatto (of African and European descent) woman who was 32 when she became literate in the Campaign while housing a female Conrado Benítez *brigadista*. She had lived her entire life in and near Playa Larga, Matanzas. She described living conditions before the triumph of the Revolution: "We lived in a small house called a *rancho* – walls of guano [a cement-like substance made from the excrement of sea birds] and a floor of dirt and charcoal. We barely survived making charcoal, and I cleaned the bosses' houses." Those bosses left for other countries after the triumph of the Revolution. Teresa also explained that there were no medical services available before the Revolution. She gave birth to six children, all with the help of her mother. She also told her memories of escaping from falling bombs in the Bay of Pigs invasion in the back of a truck in a pile of people. An elderly woman and her daughter whom she knew as neighbors died in the attacks. Later, she told me how life changed after the triumph of the Revolution and especially after the Campaign. There were improved roads, materials for constructing quality houses, free public schools, free visits from medical consultants, free ambulance service to free medical clinics, and art programs. Charcoal work continued but with humane conditions, hours, and compensation. Teresa continued studies that were provided at her work center until she finished sixth grade.

Later the same day I met with Marta Placeres Hernández (personal communication, August 1, 2003), also a resident of Playa Larga. She grew up without a school to attend and in oppressive poverty in a white family of *campesinos*. She learned to read and write as an 11-year-old during the early trial phase of the Campaign before the Bay of Pigs invasion. The invaders, to whom she referred as mercenaries, held her and other local residents hostage until the counter-revolutionaries' defeat was imminent. Marta knew a few of the civilians who were killed by the invaders' bombs. When I asked her what the Campaign meant to her community, to Cuba, to Latin America, and to the world, she stated

> I believe that the Campaign here never has ended. You should know that here there are many schools, that many Latin Americans study here in Cuba, and that the Campaign of this Revolution is about their sons' and daughters' studies and not only for Cubans. We offer solidarity for the needs of our brothers and sisters in other nations, and even the United States has students here in the School of Medical Sciences.

It is true that US citizens have gone to Cuba for medical studies when they had the ability but lacked the means to pay for their studies in their own country. The next chapter includes some detailed information about this.

My next interview was in the nearby town of Playa Girón with Miguel Tur López (personal communication, August 1, 2003), a white charcoal worker. He spoke of the long hours and toil of charcoal work as it was before the Revolution and concluded, "It was a lot of work – too much – but I had to do it to survive." He said that the work became easier after the triumph of the Revolution. Miguel was 25 years old when he became literate in the Campaign. He lived in a house with three co-workers and two *viejos* [elderly people]. The elderly man was not able to study, but the elderly woman was able and eager. Their instructor was a Conrado Benítez *briga-dista* whom Miguel described as "a young boy but very intelligent." They did not have enough space in their small house for lessons, so they built a small shelter that served their needs. The group learned to read and write together. After the Campaign, they moved to a new location where there was a school. Miguel finished the interview with his memories of the Bay of Pigs invasion. The invaders captured him and his co-workers and held them hostage for nearly an entire day. They were released on the condition that they would return to work with the invaders. He and the group hid overnight in a mountainside cave until they heard the noise of the battles stop. The next day they became prisoners again, but this time their captors were the militia of the Revolution. Before too long, some militia members recognized some prisoners and set the group free. Miguel and his *compañeros* used their house to keep militia members fed while the search for the defeated invaders in hiding continued for a couple weeks.

My final interview in La Cienaga was with Orfelina Alvariño George (personal communication, August 1, 2003), a white *campesina* in Playa Girón who was 17 when she became literate in the Campaign. During the night of the initial Bay of Pigs attack, she was in a car with Conrado Benítez *brigadistas*, her father, and her brother, the driver, trying to escape the danger. Her father told her brother to turn out the lights to avoid being spotted by the invaders, but her brother replied that he could not see where he was going without lights. They abandoned the car just in time before a missile destroyed it. The group walked toward the town of Playa Girón until a group of invaders captured them and held them as prisoners. Her father told the invaders that he would join them in their fight after he took his family home. The captors released the family, and Orfelina's father joined the militia of the Revolution instead.

At the time of our interview, Orfelina was serving as an elected municipal representative of the legislative body known as Poder Popular [People's Power], which I will address in Chapter Six. She also had been serving as lay judge without pay for 26 years in the municipal court, elected by her union. She stated that the Revolution had brought her opportunities to become a trusted leader de-

spite her humble upbringing. She also spoke of the opportunities
afforded to her children:

> When I was 17, I couldn't read or write. When my children were
> 17, they had finished high school. My daughter is an economist,
> and my son is an electrician. They didn't have to pay a penny for
> an education. The Revolution has placed in their hands the op-
> portunity to learn. If we had lived in an earlier time, they would
> have been illiterate like me at age seventeen.

The Revolution broke the cycle of illiteracy that had oppressed
generations of peasants. Young rural people suddenly had choices
and chances. They could continue farm work as part-owners of the
land, or they could pursue any career. Either way, they would have
opportunities to study beyond high school without material wealth
as a gate-keeping factor.

A week after my visit to La Cienaga, I was in the central part of
Cuba in a rural zone north of Trinidad, where I met with two men
who became literate in the Campaign while in their early twenties.
Both knew Pedro Lantigua, the *campesino* who was murdered along
with the Campaign instructor Manuel Ascunce by a counter-
revolutionary band in late November of 1961. First I spoke with
Eulampio Polo Romero (personal communication, August 8, 2003),
a white *campesino* who was 23 during the Campaign. He continued
to study after the Campaign when teachers came to live and work
in the remote area, but he did not finish sixth grade.

I then spoke with Osvaldo Hernández Villazón (personal communication, August 8, 2003), a white *campesino* who was 21 in 1961.
Manuel Ascunce was his instructor. He described Ascunce as a
young, 16-year-old, well prepared boy who came from Havana and
adapted well to the changes of ranch work. Osvaldo said that there
were about 60 *campesinos* in the area and nearly as many Conrado
Benítez *brigadistas* to teach them. The *brigadistas* were coached by
one woman who was a professional teacher. Osvaldo spoke at
length about living conditions for *campesinos* in the region before the
Revolution. They did not own any of the land on which they toiled.
They could not afford decent shoes and wore makeshift sandals.
The landowner paid them no money but rather vouchers for the

only store in the area, where the owner was a business partner with the landowner. All of the *campesinos* in the area were illiterate and isolated from the world beyond their small part of a mountainous territory. After the Campaign, Osvaldo went on the complete the ninth grade. He told me about how changes in the Revolution came with struggle. The counter-revolutionary bands that killed Ascunce remained in the area, and the CDRs provided vigilance against further terrorism. Osvaldo spoke of the agrarian reforms that made it possible for those who had worked the land for years to own some of it as large ranches became cooperatives. He mentioned that Venezuela currently was implementing similar reforms. When I asked Osvaldo about his feelings toward Cuba and socialism, he replied, "Socialism has given us life and has taught us that with work and struggle we can live well with all that we need."

The next day I was in Manicaragua, a small town near Santa Clara. There I had the opportunity to speak with Ámparo Fuentes Llerena and her two sons, Pedro and Carlos Brito Fuentes (personal communication, August 9, 2003). In 1961 Ámparo was 37, Pedro eight, and Mario six. This white family of *campesinos* lived in poverty without schools before the Revolution. After Ámparo gave birth to Pedro in a difficult cesarian procedure, the family could not pay the medical bills and became homeless. The Revolution enabled them to have a home again and made it possible for Ámparo to have the eight surgeries she needed. A Conrado Benítez *brigadista* named Fina taught the family in the Campaign. Ámparo's husband was often too busy with work, but he continued his studies after the Campaign ended. Of Fina she said, "She was very good in every sense, very interested, and it was almost like she had become a part of our family." Pedro spoke of the constant threat of counter-revolutionary bands in the area, and he remembered some members by name. He also talked about Cuba's participation in the literacy campaign of Nicaragua and the current one in Venezuela. The condensed milk that Cubans brought to Nicaragua in the 80s was for many families the first time their children had milk to drink. Pedro became an engineer and teacher, and Mario became a fiction writer. They credited the Revolution for their opportunities to have a post-secondary education.

I later spoke with another *alfabetizado* in Manicaragua named Mario Escalante Martínez (personal communication, August 9, 2003). He spoke of the difficult life before the Revolution: "The country was in bad condition, we were poor, and there was work available only half of the year." A white *campesino* at age 24 in the Campaign, he was taught by a black, female Conrado Benítez *brigadista*. He stated that he and his wife never had a problem concerning her gender or ethnicity. Their 16-year-old teacher, named Yolanda, worked with a second family as well. Mario continued his studies after the Campaign, going to classes at night or on Saturdays, until he finished ninth grade. His education allowed him to become a leader of an agricultural cooperative.

My final trip from Havana was to Consolación, a mid-sized city in Cuba's eastern-most province called Pinar del Rio. There I held a focus group with four *alfabetizados*. The woman's name was Flora Ferro, and the three men were Benito Márquez Reina, Velidio Morales, and José Hernández Altiago (personal communication, August 15, 2003). All four were white *campesinos*. Flora did not continue her studies after the Campaign, but she expressed gratitude to the Revolution for her opportunity to begin reading and writing. She talked about the misery that she and her family experienced before the Revolution and about the changes afterward that allowed her husband to become a leader among charcoal workers before retiring with security. José was 24 during the Campaign. His father raised him in a mountainous area with no school nearby, and they worked the land together. He went on to complete the sixth grade. Of his children he said, "[They] were born around the time of the triumph of the Revolution, and they are rich, meaning they have studied since pre-school." Benito was 19 when he became literate in the Campaign. He remembered the names of the two Conrado Benítez *brigadistas* from Havana who taught him along with his grandfather and a guest. Benito continued his studies through the seventh grade. Velidio was 26 in 1961. He joined neighbors in building a rustic school where all people in the vicinity could study. He described his relationship with the *brigadistas*:

"They were like brothers, and after 40 years they still come to visit us. They are family, complete brothers." Veladio continued his studies through the sixth grade. All four spoke about knowing nothing about the history of Cuba until the Campaign.

I later had an interview just outside of Consolación with an elderly woman named Alfreda Marques Ruis (personal communication, August 15, 2003), a white *campesina* who was 42 when she became literate in 1961. Her husband, a tobacco worker, died two years after the Campaign, and she raised her 11 children alone. She spoke of times before the Revolution in which her husband never was paid by the landowner for his work. After the triumph of the Revolution, her family became part-owners of the same land in a tobacco cooperative.

The *brigadista* named Ubaldo, who taught Alfreda and others in the family to read and write, was still visiting her at the end of every year and sometimes up to three times a year. She showed us a picture of him that was taken years after the Campaign. She was too busy raising children alone to continue formal studies, but all of her 11 children finished the ninth grade or higher. She asked me whether I would have taught in the Campaign if I had been a Cuban teenager in 1961. I replied in my limited but improving Spanish that I would have welcomed the opportunity for such an adventure.

My visit to Consolación also included a meeting with a family at the porch of their house. They were white *campesinos* who had a small tobacco farm. Those participating were Paulina Robaina; her sister Ana Gloria Robaina; Eladio Raúl Pagarizabal, the husband of Ana Gloria; and Raúl Pagarizabal, the son of Ana Gloria and Eladio (personal communication, August 15, 2003). During the Campaign, Paulina became literate at age 30, and Ana Gloria volunteered at age 24 as a popular literacy teacher. Eladio, a tobacco worker who was 29 in 1961, began to learn how to read and write during the Campaign at a nearby school. Raúl, an accountant, was only four during the Campaign and did not remember anything about it, but he recalled many stories that his parents and aunt had told him. He often heard them talk of the young engineer and his wife who became as close as family while they served as Conrado

Benítez *brigadistas*. The couple stayed in contact with the family long after the Campaign, but advanced age was keeping them from continuing their visits. Paulina was working as a housewife at the time of the Campaign. She did not continue her studies after 1961 because she became busier with more children. Eladio could not remember exactly but believed that he completed fourth grade. Ana Gloria spoke of her admiration of the students she taught during the Campaign. They were a family of *campesinos* who worked very hard during the day but still found the energy to learn how to read and write. The father was in his 60s, and he worked and studied with the rest.

Most of the *alfabetizados* with whom I spoke were advanced in age, the oldest being Alfreda Marques Ruis at age eighty-four. I cannot begin to imagine their lives before the Campaign. To be illiterate while living in a society with written language is to be powerless. Not all of these people I met continued their studies after the Campaign, but even a first-grade level of literacy was a significant gain. They learned the value of education and passed that value onto the next generation. The *alfabetizados*, as much as their teachers, became national heroes in Cuba's educational Revolution.

Conrado Benítez brigadistas

The young people, mostly teenagers, who traveled far to teach in the Campaign were at an age in which adventure is often appealing. Young people crave opportunities to escape from the routine and to explore the world around them, and such craving was a motivation for many young Cubans to become Conrado Benítez *brigadistas* (hereafter, referred to as "CBBs"). In addition, and foremost in many cases, there was the drive to contribute to the Revolution. Most of the CBBs were too young to fight in the war against Batista, but in 1961 they took the opportunity to fight in the war against illiteracy. I have testimonies of 24 CBBs from my interviews and focus groups of 2003. Each had fascinating stories to tell, but with some difficulty I will limit my work here to highlight the stories of twelve. The following communications, unless otherwise noted, occurred in Havana.

One of my first interviews was with Olga de la Caridad Salas Boffil (personal communication, July 13, 2003). She is a mulatto woman from a working-class *campesino* family that lived in a sugar-growing region of Oriente, the easternmost province. Her family moved to the mountainous Sierra Maestra region when she was very young. At the time of our interview she was working as a medical doctor in Havana. Olga turned 15 during her work as a CBB. She said that she had been well aware of the political meaning the Campaign from its beginning. Her mother had contributed to the clandestine support movement for the Revolution during the war, and her brothers fought in the Rebel Army. Becoming a CBB was Olga's chance to contribute. She went to a coffee-growing region to teach a family, and during the days she worked along with the family in cultivating the crop. She described the poverty of the family and their rural location: "There was no electricity, no water; houses were in bad condition because the Cuban peasants of that period still struggled to survive in the conditions of the legacy of capitalist life." She spoke of great sacrifice in her work but also of tremendous rewards. The family responded well to her teaching. At the end of the Campaign she was deeply saddened to leave them, and she was in tears as she told me about her departure. She was still in contact with the family. The couple, who were in their fifties during the Campaign, had died, but she was still in touch with their children and grandchildren.

Olga took full advantage of the government's scholarship offered to CBBs after the campaign, and she became a medical doctor. She stated, "I am a doctor thanks to the Campaign, which was something that moved to maturity my idea to carry health and life to those villages and those human beings." Her oldest daughter followed her path and was working as a medical doctor for the neediest people in Panamá. Olga expressed hope for the Bolivarian Revolution of Venezuela and its current national literacy campaign, and she was ready to go there if the need for more international volunteers would arise.

A few days later I was interviewing a mother and daughter who both served as CBBs in Pinar del Rio. Nancy Virginia Palacio was 13 in 1961, and her mom, María Virginia Martínez (personal communication, July 17, 2003), was thirty-nine. They are white women who had a middle-class life in Havana before the Revolution. María, a sixth-grade teacher of adults, was married to a Presbyterian minister. When I asked whether they were involved in the Revolutionary War against Batista, Nancy replied that they hid their support for Castro because the church was about equally divided between those for and those against the Revolution. Some church members were killed by Batista's army, and others were soldiers in it. She reiterated, "Even though we didn't participate directly, we supported Fidel."

Nancy and María worked together with the same extended family. They talked about a typical day in the Campaign. After breakfast, they taught the housewives. Later in the morning and after lunch, they helped them with their chores. Literacy lessons then continued after chores were done. After bathing and dinner, Nancy and María taught the men, who had been working the land all day. One of the men was deaf-mute, and he participated in the learning. María said, "I felt very important seeing that I could help a person who couldn't speak learn to read and write. He would return from the grocery store and write for me what he had bought." Before long, the two visiting women felt like they were part of the family. Their student-hosts grew up believing that they would never get the opportunity to learn how to read and write. Nancy recalled, "At first they thought that [becoming literate] was impossible at their age, but when they realized that they actually were learning, they were filled with immense joy." Nancy also spoke of hearing news about counter-revolutionary bands that were not far away. Fortunately, these bands never stopped the progress of the Campaign in Pinar del Río. After the Campaign, María returned to her work of teaching sixth grade to adults. Nancy completed her studies and used her CBB scholarship to become an English teacher. When I asked whether the Campaign was a mass movement of civic education, Nancy explained that bringing literacy to all Cubans was a point of departure for a new civic education. She and her mother both spoke of their hopes that the current national literacy campaign in Venezuela would succeed.

Next I met Clara Josefa Bernal Hernández (personal communication, July 19, 2003), a black woman who was a CBB at age twelve. With her during the interview was her father, a retired truck driver. Clara was proud of her accomplishments, including several rewards for her work as a chemical engineer. Her son also had become an engineer. She was growing up in the province of Camagüey, and her teaching assignment for the Campaign was in a more rural part of Camagüey. She successfully taught four people, and then six more. She spoke of some hardships in dealing with the poverty in the rural zone; however, she said, "My personal sacrifice was nothing compared to all the happiness that I received when seeing the smile on an elderly student or on a child." Some of Clara's students were Haitian immigrants, and she taught them in Spanish successfully as well. In return she learned a few things from her students: how to take care of a cow, how to sweep a dirt floor, how to cook certain meals, and how to crochet. I asked her what the Campaign meant for Cuba, and she replied, "We are a country that has education, that knows what we want and where we are going, and that can determine that nobody will deceive us because we know primordially how to read and write." At the end of the interview I asked Clara if there was something more she wanted to say. She graciously stated, "Take this interview as something real. I speak for the desire to help in the understanding of the thesis of a man whom I have just met, who is *norteamericano*, a human being, and, as such, deserves my help."

My next interview was with a married couple, both university professors of pedagogy, and both of whom served as CBBs in the Campaign. Mireida Pérez Marrero was 13 in 1961, and her husband, Sergio Pérez Benítez (personal communication, July 20, 2003), was fifteen. She was from a white *campesino* family in Holguín province, and he was from a white middle-class family in Havana. Sergio's parents refused to sign the permission form, so he forged a signature and ran off to the training center for CBBs in Varadero. Sergio said that his parents refused to sign not in opposition to the Revolution but rather out of fear that something bad might hap-

pen. His father tried to find him in Varadero, but Sergio was already on a train to Guantánamo for his teaching assignment. His
father found him at a train stop in Santa Clara. Upon seeing Sergio's determination to work in the Campaign, he changed his mind
and gave his permission for Sergio to keep going eastward. Ironi-
cally, something bad did happen to Sergio. He fell off of a horse
and was unconscious for ten days, and headaches continued to give
him problems to the present. Still he was glad for all that he learned
about rural life and for his chance to be a part of the Campaign.

Mireida had an easier time adjusting to her surroundings because she was from a rural area. She helped with work in the fields
as well as in the house. I asked the couple whether they thought of
the Campaign as a mass movement of civic education, and both
agreed that it was. Mireida saw it as something more, though:
"Many Cubans believe that it [the Campaign] was a movement of
popular education and was a movement among the most important
in Cuba for having been made by people such as youth, and so well
defined and well outlined." As I explained in Chapter Four, "popular education" was not a phrase that had been coined before 1961,
but the Campaign arguably provides a telling example of the concept.

I was conducting interviews almost every day in July, but I took
a break on the 26th. That was the 50th anniversary of the attack on
the Moncada barracks, Cuba's most celebrated event in history. I
joined the celebration held at Luís' and Loly's apartment. Among
the guests were Felipe and his family. We had the television on
when Fidel Castro spoke in Santiago at the large ceremony honoring the survivors and the martyrs of the seminal attack that sparked
the Revolution. Cuba's July 26 was as big as July 4 in the US.
There were no fireworks, but people decorated the outside of their
homes to honor the Revolution.

I returned to my busy schedule of interviews and met with
Gladys Bermello Lastra (personal communication, July 28, 2003).
Her small apartment, which she shared with her husband, had a
rather large library. She was from a white, middle-class family in
Havana and had attended a private school. Her father was director
of cinematography for a television station. After the triumph of the

Revolution, Gladys joined an organization called the Revolutionary Students of Private Schools, which was assisted by the Association of Rebel Youth. Her parents had contributed money to the Rebel Army during the war and had attended the secret meetings of the Popular Socialist Party. Her family joined the celebrations in the streets following the triumph of the Revolution. Gladys became a CBB at age 17 at about the time that private schools were nationalized. She was her parents' only child, but they were glad to sign her permission form for the Campaign. She arrived at Playa Girón three days before the Bay of Pigs invasion. I asked her how the attack affected her, and she replied, "It affected me as a revolutionary and offended me as a patriot, as a member of this country, which we don't consider open for anyone from the outside to tell us what it is and what we must do."

Gladys spoke at length about the hardships and sacrifices that she experienced in the harsh rural conditions – dirt floors, lack of latrines and electricity, makeshift wells, mosquitoes, and mice. She was living in a house for charcoal workers, and after the Bay of Pigs attack the workers took turns on an embankment keeping watch for signs of another invasion while carrying a rifle. Gladys knew nothing about firearms, but she volunteered time for the ongoing patrol. She taught a family of five that included a 60-year-old woman who had been able to read and write in her youth but forgot due to lack of practice. This grandmother was her most eager student. The lessons were in the late afternoon, after the charcoal workers, who were all men, had completed their work and before the onslaught of mosquitoes. Each bed had a mosquito net. During the day, Gladys helped the women with chores in and around the house. After the Campaign, she studied Russian language and literature. Her college education included two years in the Soviet Union. She went on to complete a doctorate in philosophy in 1983 through correspondence courses from Moscow. Also, through the years she continued to work on her English. She has taught languages and pedagogy at different levels. She stated that the Campaign was a triumph not only for the Revolution but also for humanity. Among her last words of the interview were these: "[Cubans] have a scholarship level now that is a result of the work of those who had been able to teach, and for Latin America and the world the Campaign provides an example that it can be done."

Felipe, Julio and I traveled to Trinidad to conduct a focus group of ten people who had been involved in the Campaign in various ways. One of the most memorable testimonies came from María Cantero Mendoza (personal communication, August 7, 2003), a black woman who was 12 years old in 1961. Her father signed her 14-year-old sister's consent form for becoming a CBB but refused to sign hers, believing that she was too young. María responded with an ultimatum: she would not eat until she had her father's signature. On the second day of the hunger strike her father signed the form, and within days María was at the training camp in Varadero. She taught seven *campesinos* how to read and write, but she also spoke of how much she learned from the women about managing a home. Her excitement for teaching and learning in the Campaign was interrupted with tragedy. Her location was near the site where fellow-CBB Manuel Ascunce was murdered. For several days the CBBs of the area wore civilian clothes instead of their uniforms out of fear that the counter-revolutionary bands might target more teachers. María recalled that nobody in the area abandoned the work of the Campaign and that her municipality went on to celebrate a successful finish. She went to Havana for the grand celebration of the Campaign and with other CBBs chanted to Fidel Castro a phrase asking what they could do next. Her parents were tremendously proud of her accomplishments. Before allowing the next participant of the focus group to speak, she ended her brief testimony with these words about her return home: "My mother told everyone who visited the house how I had been able to teach with my young age and small stature, and it was a delight...the years pass and still it's a delight to talk of that Campaign."

Another focus group took place in Manicaragua, a town near Santa Clara. Mercedes Águila Ordanivia (personal communication, August 8, 2003), a retired teacher of Spanish literature, was among the six participants. I do not remember her face, but the transcripts of her testimony reveal how courageous young Cubans were. Mercedes was 15 when she was a CBB in the mountainous Escambray region, where many counter-revolutionary bands were known to be

stationed. She recalled hearing airplanes after learning about the
Bay of Pigs invasion, and she did not know whose planes they were.
Despite the dangers, she and other CBBs never thought of quitting
their work in the Campaign: "We never had fear because, when
Fidel gave us the call, we went and didn't question where we must
go or what we must do. They told us to teach; if we finished in one
house, we found another." Mercedes also spoke of finding out how
a man whom she taught in the Campaign was later found to be in
cooperation with the bands: "I felt chills... [The family] loved me so
much, and then he was in prison. When he left prison, I visited him
because he was so thankful for me, and I for him...Later he died."
Felipe then commented, "It's interesting because you're saying that
there was literacy instruction without asking whether one sympa-
thized with the Revolution. We gave the service of the Campaign to
all Cubans...We only asked whether they wanted to learn to read
and write." Julio added, "There was no ideology test." Mercedes
went on to say that one of the beautiful legacies of the Campaign
was how Cubans later participated in literacy campaigns in Nicaragua and parts of Africa.

When we left Manicaragua, we went to Santa Clara to visit the
mausoleum of Che Guevara. His remains were moved from Bolivia
to Cuba in 1997, and upon their arrival Fidel Castro spoke at a
ceremony at the site of the mausoleum. There were many visitors
from around the world when we were there. When we finished seeing the monuments to Guevara and the rebels who died with him
in Bolivia, I interviewed the director of the mausoleum, who was a
CBB at age twelve. Mercedes Piñón Jareño (personal communication, August 8, 2003) is a white woman with a middle-class upbringing in the eastern province of Las Tunas. She began the interview
speaking of Guevara, of how people need to demystify him and see
him as a human being. She gave a brief history of his leadership
role in literacy work from the Cuban Revolutionary War to the
guerrilla revolts in the Congo and Bolivia. Later, Mercedes talked
of her experience as a CBB. She was an only child, and her father
was a sugar worker who had attained a standard of living high
enough to send her to a private school. He helped the Rebel Army
during the war, as did most families that Mercedes recalled. After

the training in Varadero, she lived with a family in a rural zone of Las Tunas. They had very little land and made ends meet by making charcoal. She recalled how a professional teacher had to keep her and other "immature" CBBs in control. She began teaching an elderly *campesino* who lived in a more remote area, and she spoke of the adventure of learning how to ride a horse in order to visit him. Later, she taught three more elderly people and five young people. She stayed in touch with her students after the Campaign, and one of the young ones became a medical technician. Mercedes was hopeful that the current literacy campaign in Venezuela would succeed. She ended the interview saying, "Hopefully, one day all nations that are of the Third World, and also those that are not, will have a citizenry completely literate. For me that was one of the most beautiful accomplishments of this Revolution."

After returning to Havana, I spoke with Percy Francisco Alvarado Godoy (personal communication, August 13, 2003). Born in Guatemala, his family fled to Argentina after the reactionary forces supported by the US government overthrew the Arbenz administration in 1954. The family then moved to Cuba after the 1959 triumph of the Revolution, and Percy became a CBB near Playa Girón at age twelve. He became part of an organized network of international volunteers in the National Literacy Campaign. He stated in the interview that, among the foreign CBBs with whom he had stayed in contact, not a single one had rejected the Revolution. Percy said that there were many of them from many countries, including the US.

During his adulthood, Percy had spent 22 years in Miami infiltrating the National Federation of Cuban Americans, a counterrevolutionary organization that had been involved in terrorism against the Cuban Revolution. He did not feel that the Cuban Americans were enemies but rather human beings caught in an historical conflict. Regarding the Campaign and global citizenship, he said, "Solidarity between human beings is what I learned in poverty and in wealth, because I am a wealthy man. We are all wealthy people. The Literacy Campaign helped instill in me a sense of solidarity with other people." He went on to speak of how discrimination can unite the oppressed against an oppressor. His words made me think of how the Campaign helped to dismantle the traditional discriminations against rural people, women, and Afro-Cubans. For the first time in Cuban history, literacy became a human right for all without exceptions. Furthermore, the participation of foreign CBBs demonstrated how human solidarity is stronger than political borders. This is the essence of critical global citizenship.

A final CBB whom I wish to include here is Sergio Ballester Pedroso (personal communication, July 25, 2003). Sergio, a professor of pedagogy, is black with a working-class upbringing. He was 12 in 1961. I interviewed him following his wife, Elina Hernandez Galarraga, who was a popular literacy teacher. Although he was so young, Sergio was determined to do what he could to defend the Revolution against aggression: "If I could not defend the Revolution with arms, then I was going with pencils. I joined the Campaign late. Although without the consent of my mother, my father signed my consent form." He taught militia in the province of Camagüey. With his small stature, he became the "pet" of the troops and the object of good-natured jokes and games. Sergio also spent one month teaching militia on a tiny island that is part of the Cuban archipelago. He and other CBBs participated in many of the regimens of the militia during a typical day, including training in the use of arms.

Sergio spoke at length with me about global citizenship. He stated that citizenship is a matter of belonging to one's region or nation, but he also emphasized the importance of becoming "patriots of the world, of being at the point of having conscience of global problems that we can resolve." He spoke of building the capacity to think about the "grand homeland" as a necessary part of civic education. He gave an example of AIDS as a global problem: "We have to work on that and not work only for Cubans. We have to work to eradicate that from humanity. We need to try to reduce it not only in one country but rather in all of them."

Sergio's words go to the heart of critical global citizenship. There are many global problems that will not be resolved until a critical mass develops a conscience of them and a political will to mobilize against them. AIDS is preventable, and its devastation can be diminished with education for critical global citizenship. Although there is no cure, there are treatments that can lengthen and improve the lives of persons with HIV. Millions suffer without such treatments because there is a lack of global political will to make them available. The capitalist market cynically determines the value of human lives, and the proliferation of AIDS in "Third World" countries continues to cause human suffering that is preventable. This is nothing short of a crime against humanity, and critical global citizens are those who understand this and act.

Popular literacy teachers

The CBBs are the most legendary members of the teaching force in the Campaign, but the contributions of the popular literacy teachers were critical to the national mission as well. The popular literacy teachers taught their neighbors in cities and towns while continuing to live in their own homes. Many of them were adolescents or pre-adolescents who wanted to teach but did not receive parental consent to become CBBs. I have testimonies of more than a dozen popular literacy teachers, and here I will feature only four. "Popular literacy teacher" is a translation from *alfabetizador popular* in Spanish, and hereafter I will use the Spanish acronym "AP."

Elina Hernández Galarraga (personal communication, July 25, 2003), like her husband Sergio Ballester Pedroso, is a professor of pedagogy. She is black with a middle-class upbringing, and she was an AP in the Campaign at age twelve. When the nationalization of private schools occurred, the one she attended adopted the name "Victims of the Coubre" to commemorate casualties on March 4, 1960, when counter-revolutionaries exploded the French ship carrying Belgian arms, killing 72 Cubans and injuring two hundred. Elina wanted to be a CBB, and she cried when her mother refused to grant permission. Her father took her with him to work in the census of illiterate people in their hometown of Cárdenas, Matanzas, and later she became an AP. She became frustrated when one man had great difficulty learning to write, but neither she nor the man gave up. He successfully completed the work, including a short letter to Castro with large, dark handwriting. When I asked Elina

what the Campaign meant to Cuba and to the world, she replied,
"I think that we were an example of what can be accomplished
with great political will." She said that many international observers
of the Campaign thought that the idea of eliminating illiteracy in a
year was crazy but that the Cuban people proved them wrong with
their conviction and hard work. She stated also that the report on
the Campaign by UNESCO gave credibility to the Revolution and
Castro's leadership.

Raúl Pérez Rivero (personal communication, July 12, 2003), a
math professor in a long teaching career, was only ten when he became an AP. I had the pleasure of getting to know Raúl because he
drove his car a few times to take me to some of my interviews in
Havana. He is white and was raised in a working-class family. His
mother was a second-generation strong revolutionary, and his father was apolitical. After the Campaign, he helped his father in the
continuation program called the Battle for the Sixth Grade. Raúl
taught every night Monday through Friday and every Saturday
morning during the entire Campaign in the house of a family of
three adults near his home in Havana. He said that his neighborhood was poor but that there were electric lights. He recalled that
one family member struggled with vision and that there was a delay
in the delivery of glasses. In the end everyone had learned successfully. Given his young age in 1961, many of his memories of the
Campaign were blurred. Still, he recalled that his students were
grateful to have the opportunity to become literate. Raúl became a
member of his neighborhood's Committee in Defense of the Revolution while still a teenager and credited his willingness to participate to the sense of purpose that he gained during the Campaign.
When asked what the Campaign meant for his community, Cuba,
and the world, Raúl first stated that only literate people can participate in a country's development. Then he turned his attention to
Venezuela and the current national literacy campaign there: "Today Venezuela at least has our reference and our experience from
things written about our Campaign. I think that we established
guidelines in this sense and that that has been an example for the
whole world." Raúl also shared that his own sense of global citizenship moved him to teach twice during his career in Africa.

There are two more APs whom I want to highlight. Ofelia Al-
fonso Álvarez (personal communication, July 15, 2003), a retired
economist, grew up in a white working-class family in Havana. At
age 16 in 1961, she wanted to become a CBB, but her parents refused to give consent. She joined her father in teaching a family of
five adults living nearby. One student asked for extra lessons on
Sundays, and Ofelia gladly agreed to give them to him. Another AP
was Gladys Hernández Solana (personal communication, July 15,
2003), a biology professor who was raised in a white middle-class
family in Havana. She was 13 when she joined her mother in teaching hospital patients. They experienced a high turnover of students,
but their contribution illustrates how the Campaign strived to serve
everyone in need without delay.

Patria o Muerte Brigadistas

The workers who became literacy teachers later in the Campaign were called *Brigadistas Patria o Muerte* [Homeland or Death
Troops], and I had only two interviews with them. One was with
Pedro "Peglez" Gonzalez (personal communication, July 22, 2003).
Pedro had a working-class upbringing and was a 19-year-old white
journalist and poet in Havana in 1961. He had taught soldiers of
the Rebel Army during the war and had become a leader of the
Rebel Youth after the Revolution's triumph. He became an instructor in the Campaign in the easternmost province of Oriente within
a group of instructors from the transportation union. They taught
in a mountainous coffee-growing region and helped with the farm
work during the days. Pedro stated that Venezuela was not copying
Cuba in its current literacy campaign but that it was becoming "a
new country with new possibilities." He concluded by saying that
Cuba's Campaign made history for Latin America and for the underdeveloped world.

My other interview with a *Patria o Muerte brigadista* was with
Roberto Abreu García (personal communication, July 25, 2003), a
retired shoemaker who had been a union official. Roberto did not
fight in the war, but he participated in the urban underground support network. A mulatto man from a working-class childhood,

Roberto became an instructor in the Campaign at age twenty-three. He became a supervisor of instructors and taught two of his co-workers in the shoe factory in Santa Clara. He began his testimony with descriptions of working conditions before and after the Revolution's triumph: "Shoemakers had great misery, and the Revolution gave us so much help. It brought new tariffs, raised salaries by more than 50 percent, and provided security for full-time work." He talked of how the economic blockade by the US closed down much of his factory in 1962 due to the cut supply of raw materials. Laid-off workers received support from the Cuban government to return to school in preparation for different work. One of Roberto's students in the Campaign was still working in the shoe factory. After the Campaign, Roberto finished his degree in social sciences at a university for adults while he continued working in the factory. His framed diploma was displayed in a prominent place on the wall in his apartment, and I took his photo next to it. His smile told more of his satisfaction than words could ever express.

Additional roles in the Campaign

There were numerous roles in the Campaign that involved duties other than direct learning and teaching. Many workers drove trucks and built bridges so that CBBs could arrive safely to the rural zones where they would teach. Volunteers helped in the census of illiterate people. Professional teachers mentored all instructors. People with fundraising or accounting experience helped to organize the finances for the Campaign. Educational leaders became the administrators at municipal, provincial, and national levels. As mentioned in the previous chapter, the Integrated Revolutionary Organizations (ORIs) and the local Committees in Defense of the Revolution (CDRs) volunteered in many ways to contribute their energies. Here I will highlight five individuals who filled some of these roles—a transportation worker, two professional teachers, an administrator, and a volunteer assistant.

José Hortelio Acosta Fernández (personal communication, August 8, 2003), a white man, was 24 when he served the Campaign as a transportation worker. He helped CBBs arrive at their hosts' homes, and he transported people and goods as necessary throughout the Campaign. His testimony, the last in the focus group at Trinidad, was the most emotional moment of all the interviews and focus groups that I conducted. He had to stop and cry as he explained how he was the one who had to cut the rope from which Manuel Ascunce's body was hanging. He had known both of the counter-revolutionaries' victims—Ascunce the CBB and Pedro Lantigua the student-host. José ended his testimony with his memory of being at the national celebration of the Campaign's end in Havana. He felt great joy as he rode in a car that carried a giant flag with the words "Escambray, territory free of illiteracy." He said that the Campaign was the greatest achievement of the Revolution, and he also expressed his pride that Cubans were contributing to other literacy campaigns: "And so we have Venezuela, and Ecuadorans already came to sign a project with Cuba involving literacy. I think that later we will arrive in Brazil, and we will give birth of literacy to all nations that call us." He added that Cubans are friends of the people of all nations, including the US, and are full of hope for peace.

One afternoon in Havana I had the opportunity to visit a neighborhood activity center for elderly people, and there I interviewed a married couple, both retired elementary teachers. Both served in the Campaign as supervisors of instructors, or *asesores técnicas* [technical assessors]. I interviewed Josefa Larralde Pineda (personal communication, July 24, 2003) first. A white woman with a working-class childhood, she was 34 in 1961. She had not been involved in the Revolutionary War, but her brother was tortured. Batista's police suspected that she and her husband were clandestine supporters of the Revolution, and the couple knew that they were being watched closely. After the triumph of the Revolution, Josefa left her urban job in Sancti Spíritus to spend time teaching in the mountainous Escambray region, where there had been no schools. That was where she later supervised CBBs in the Campaign. She gave orientations to the new CBBs and to their host families, letting the young instructors know that she expected them to respect their elders as a son or daughter would a parent. Josefa guided the CBBs in the use of the primer as needed. Even though there were threats from counter-revolutionary bands, nobody among instructors abandoned the Campaign. All of their students learned, including the most elderly. Josefa knew Manuel Ascunce from provincial meetings, where she remembered that the 16-year-old CBB gave impressive presentations on political economy. I asked Josefa to talk of civics education before the Revolution, and she spoke of a teacher: "The teacher I had was communist, Dr. Jorge Gaspar García Galló. He gave magnificent civic lessons, and he was a representative in congress. I visited his house also in Santa Clara. He was fantastic." When I asked her what the Campaign meant for Cuba, Latin America, and the world, she stated the following: "Hopefully in Latin America and the world there will be one great literacy campaign...Many are illiterate, and people exploit them without scruples because they can take advantage of their ignorance." She ended by saying that she wished I could have seen how helpless peasants before the Revolution lost their land and their livelihoods.

I then interviewed Josefa's husband, Manuel Hernández Santana Casanova (personal communication, July 24, 2003). A mulatto man from a tobacco-working family in Sancti Spíritus, Manuel was 40 when he became a supervisor in the Campaign. In 1946 a rural community of *campesinos* refused to allow Manuel to become a teacher. Manuel explained, "After several days, the *campesino* told me, 'We are not interested in learning to read and write, and besides, they don't accept you.' I asked why, and he pointed at my skin because I was mulatto." These landless peasants had gone three years without a teacher in their small school, yet due to racial prejudice they refused the services of an able teacher who was willing to work without pay for only the same food that they ate and was willing to sleep on the school floor. Manuel later became active in the Popular Socialist Party while teaching in a private elementary school in Havana and completing a doctorate in pedagogy. In the Campaign he mentored 12 APs and did some teaching of two domestic workers in Miramar, the part of Havana where many foreign ambassadors' families lived. He touched on themes of critical global citizenship at different points of the interview. Manuel claimed that Cubans are not *anti-norteamericanos* [anti-US] but rather are anti-imperialist and that sovereignty is the right of all nations. He stated that Cuba is not trying to "Cubanize" Venezuela but that Cuba will always be ready to send doctors and educators to countries that are in transformation to meet the needs of people. Of the Campaign he concluded that Cuba provides an example for Latin America and other countries that have many people who are "without the light of literacy."

A final interview that I wish to highlight is that with Juan Luís Báez Martínez and Emilia Ortiz Romo (personal communication, July 27, 2003), also a married couple. I interviewed them together on the front porch of their old wooden house in Madruga, a small city in the province of Havana. A white man with a middle-class upbringing, Juan became a successful owner of two businesses – an electronics firm affiliated with Esso Standard Oil and a funeral home. Emilia, white and from a working-class family, raised the couple's four children. During the war, Juan participated with the clandestine movement in support of the Rebel Army. Upon the Revolution's triumph, he was among the first to voluntarily hand over businesses to nationalization. Fidel Castro once visited the couple in their home and expressed the importance of Juan's ability to repair firearms for the militia.

During the Campaign, Juan was president of the Municipal Literacy Council of Madruga in the province of Havana. Emilia assisted him and went to Oriente four times to help her daughter, who was a CBB there. In Madruga Juan and Emilia temporarily housed CBBs and assigned them to rural families in need of instruction. Emilia told me how two black female *brigadistas* were at first rejected by prospective host families because of racism: "A man told [Juan] that they didn't want black people in the house because the daughters were afraid of them, and [Juan] put one there and another next door…Later they were extremely satisfied with the black girls."

Juan had an additional anecdote that is worth quoting at length:

When I went to Varadero to bring *brigadistas*, they told me that there almost weren't any because almost all they had were black girls. And then I told them that I would take all above age 10 that needed placement, and they told me that was the exception because nobody wants black girls. And I told them, "I am going to take all of them." And I took 19, all older than twelve, and the director of the Campaign there congratulated me because he says that that had never happened before, that someone would request black girls. I took them to a zone where they were terrified of black people, and I placed them in that zone. And after the Campaign ended, [the *brigadistas*] continued visiting those families, and the families visited them in Havana because they all remained delighted as if they were family. I united blacks and whites because they are equal. (As quoted in Abendroth, 2005, pp. 99-100)

Racism in Cuba before 1959 reflected the same in the U.S. Afro-Cubans faced widespread legal discrimination. The Revolution's triumph brought a sudden end to *de jure* racial segregation in Cuba. Like the US, Cuba has not eliminated *de facto* racial segregation and discrimination. However, unlike the US, Cuba has developed a common belief that proletarian and nationalist identities and struggles are factors working to unite the nation. The inclusiveness of the Literacy Campaign advanced that belief.

Juan and Emilia are among several Cubans I interviewed who committed what Amílcar Cabral (1970) called class suicide. Before the triumph of the Revolution, they enjoyed a very comfortable upper-middle-class lifestyle. However, he had joined the clandestine operations of the July 26 Movement and had to flee to the US for his safety. The US then deported him to Ecuador. His wife and children took care of the businesses until the triumph. Instead of taking his wealth to the United States, he willingly yielded his businesses to nationalization.

Concluding thoughts on the testimonies

Even if one does not believe in the Revolution's tenets of national sovereignty, egalitarianism, and international solidarity, it

must be difficult to deny the greatness of what Cuba accomplished
in the National Literacy Campaign. It is among the world's most
important accomplishments in education in the 20th Century, and
yet it is such a little-known fact of Cuba in the tunnel vision of US
citizens. I was a curious *norteamericano* trying to uncover this historical Cuban project in order to better understand how an economically distressed country in Latin America could pull off such an
ambitious endeavor in so little time. I had difficulty imagining how
a country with nearly a quarter of its population being illiterate
could reduce that figure to below four percent within a single year
(Lorenzetto & Neys, 1965).

The Campaign did not happen miraculously. It needed leadership, mass mobilization, and a great deal of hard work. It also followed a Revolution. The Revolution followed pre-revolutionary
conditions, which were the outcome of centuries of subjugation under colonial and neocolonial rule. The people whose testimonies I
gathered have experienced life in Cuba before and after the triumph of the Revolution, and they believe that they and the majority of Cubans have better lives in the Revolution. They could not
speak of the Campaign without speaking of the Revolution, and
vice versa. Their testimonies collectively spoke of the three themes
that I highlighted in the previous chapter – civic engagement of
youth, popular education, and critical global education. These participants of the Campaign understand deeply how the Campaign
played a pivotal role in the survival of the Revolution. Education
became the foundation by which all Cubans became not mere
stakeholders in the Revolution but also citizens capable of participating as change agents. Community organizing in the US is a
grassroots endeavor that demands great efforts with seriously limited resources. In Cuba, community organizing is a part of the national culture with the national government giving its full support.
The National Literacy Campaign made it possible for Cubans of all
ages to be involved in creating the course of the Revolution. The
legacy of the Campaign – the Revolution's ongoing commitment to
a high quality of education for all – ensures that Cubans will not
turn back to their pre-revolutionary condition without a great
struggle. An educated people are citizens who know who they are

and from where they have come. They can and do become critical
global citizens who will never again be easily subjugated by neoliberalism or by any other nation.

6. The Legacy of the Campaign

The National Literacy Campaign proved that an underdeveloped and historically overexploited nation can eradicate illiteracy on a massive scale in a short period of time. The real test, though, came in the years and decades that followed. Would the newly literate people continue to learn? Would education become a sustaining force as the Revolution continued to face adversity? Would youth continue to be engaged in educational missions of Revolutionary Cuba? Would a grassroots popular education be able to operate along with Cuba's centralized government? Would Cuban educators play a role in internationalism and critical global citizenship in Latin America and among Third World nations around the globe?

Following up

When the Campaign came to an end, Cuba had more than 707,000 citizens who had been illiterate and achieved literacy at a first-grade level. They had learned to read and write, but they needed more instruction in order to reach a level where they could participate as empowered citizens in the making and remaking of the Revolution. Elementary educators often say that a student learns to read and then, after third grade or so, reads to learn. The newly literate Cubans had learned plenty, though, in their oppressed lives before the Revolution. Their new abilities to read and write suddenly gave them opportunities to find their experiences in historical context and to express more articulately who they were and who they wanted to become.

The Cuban government continued to invest heavily in 1962 in the human capital of education for adults as well as youth. The first courses of the *Seguimiento* [follow-up] program for adults started on February 24 (Lorenzetto & Neys, 1965). The Ministry of Education created the Department of Worker-Farmer Education to address the specific needs of adult learners. Several priorities for education

were in place at the end of the Literacy Campaign. Science education became the government's hope for economic development,
and the schools-in-the-countryside program began as an intentional
policy to bridge the gap between rural and urban education. Before
the end of 1962, the *Seguimiento* program took the new name of the
"Battle for the Sixth Grade." Newly literate adults attended courses
with the goal of completing at least an elementary education, and
more than 500,000 of them graduated from the sixth grade by 1973
(Canfux, 1981). Meanwhile, the primary and secondary schools for
youth were finding their places in society after the 1961 nationalization of all private schools. School councils became separate from
the Ministry of Education, thereby linking people in local communities more directly with the schools (Lutjens, 1996). The municipal
councils that had been so instrumental in the work of the Literacy
Campaign were taking leadership in the local schools.

Education in phases of the Revolution

Since 1962, the Cuban Revolution has undergone changes
while staying focused on its socialist and emancipatory-nationalist
orientations. Education, in turn, has changed at different points in
time to support the changing strategies. The greatest changes came
with increased Soviet influence in many aspects of the Revolution
and then with the effects on Cuba of the Soviet Union's collapse.
Changes continue today with Cuba re-inventing its socialism in the
post-Cold War global momentum of neoliberalism.

Throughout 1962, and especially after the October missile crisis, Cuban education took a bolder turn toward promoting socialism. The Schools of Revolutionary Instruction (EIR for the Spanish
acronym) had been conceived secretly in late 1960 for selected elementary and secondary schools, and they were implemented in
January of 1961 (Fagen, 1968). This was before Castro's declaration of the socialist nature of the Revolution, yet the project involved collaboration between the July 26 Movement and the Popular Socialist Party. These two organizations disagreed on many
ideas during the early years of the Revolution, and the July 26
Movement was not ready to publicly declare a merger of its anti-

imperialist nationalism with socialism. After Castro publicly embraced socialism for the Revolution in April of 1961, the EIRs put
socialism in a prominent place of the curriculum. These schools
existed until 1967, when the government realized that simply teaching about Marxism-Leninism did not guarantee that young people
would accept it. There was a realization that a Soviet-made curriculum was not completely helpful in Cuba's quest to build its own
identity.

A concept that has taken on central meaning in Cuba's education within the Revolution is the *new man*. Che Guevara (2003) advanced this idea in his famous 1965 essay titled "Man and socialism
in Cuba." The gender-exclusive language of that time does not
need to distract readers from Guevara's intent to include all Cuban
women as well as men in his thinking, and a recent translation into
English reflects that intent. Guevara wrote, "In this period of the
building of socialism we can see the new man and woman being
born." He explained that this rebirth process would never end as it
"goes forward hand in hand with the development of new economic forms" (p. 218). The idea was that Cuban individuals would
have to change in order for the Revolution to be viable and sustainable.

Lidia Turner Martí, a leading Cuban scholar of pedagogy,
wrote a book titled *Del pensamiento pedagógico de Ernesto Che Guevara*
[Of the pedagogical thinking of Ernesto Che Guevara], which was
published in 1999. She explores how Guevara in his writings did
not reject individualism for a rigid collectivism in his concept of the
new man. Rather than seeing the individual and the collective in
binary terms, Guevara spoke and wrote of how the two needed to
function interdependently. A critical view of the group, in
Guevara's view, needed to develop among Cuban youth as they
prepared as individuals to be full participants in shaping their socialist society. Their diverse opinions as individual citizens would be
a source of strength for building a sense of community in neighborhoods and in the nation. Turner explains that in a capitalist society
the individual fundamentally learns to look out for one's own interests and that, by contrast, in a socialist society envisioned by

Guevara the individual learns that the love of humanity is the
greatest trait that any individual can develop.

Another important writing on Guevara's contributions to revolutionary education is in Peter McLaren's (2000) book titled *Che
Guevara, Paulo Freire, and the pedagogy of revolution*. This is an impas-
sioned call for a revolutionary critical pedagogy that takes Guevara
seriously in the present struggle against neoliberal global capitalism.
McLaren articulates how Guevara's ideas for transforming societies
are powerfully linked to the transformation of individuals and institutions, especially educational institutions. The book also looks at
how many educators have domesticated Freire by claiming to follow his problem-posing process without embracing the entire revolutionary who was Freire. Comparing the revolutionary pedagogies
of Guevara and Freire is a challenging exercise that merits careful
study, and McLaren sets the stage in this one volume.

Guevara's 1967 death in Bolivia made him a martyr and a national hero in Cuban history. Children in Cuban schools honor him
by chanting, "Pioneers for communism, we will be like Che."
Across from the monument to Martí in Havana's Revolution Plaza
a building has on its side a giant iron sculpture in lines that form the
image of Guevara's face as depicted in the world-famous photograph by Alberto Korda that was taken on March 5, 1960, the day
after the deadly bombing of the ship called the *Coubre*. Guevara is
an icon to leftists throughout Latin America and the world, but
Cubans continue to claim the Argentine native as their own. He
played a critical role in moving Castro and the July 26 Movement
to accept Marxism, and many Latin American leftists see him as an
historical nexus in advancing the struggle for regional autonomy
that was first led by Bolívar.

Cuban schools, after the 1967 demise of the EIRs, strived to
develop a curriculum and instruction more aligned with the unique
situations and goals of the Cuban Revolution. The Communist
Party of Cuba (PCC in the Spanish acronym) had formed in 1965
as an official synthesis of the July 26 Movement, the Popular Socialist Party, and what remained of the student-based Revolutionary
Directorate. These three organizations had begun the process of
uniting in 1961, when together they formed a party called the Inte-

grated Revolutionary Organizations. In 1963, the party was re-named the United Party of the Socialist Revolution. The PCC be-came the vanguard party that played a central role in Marxist the-ory regarding the socialist transformation of a nation. It exercised enormous influence in decisions on educational policy but did not become a monopoly (Lutjens, 1996). Principals, who were not re-quired to be Party members, worked with school councils in creat-ing programs for socialist and communist education.

Cuban youth organizations became an important part of de-veloping future leaders in the Revolution. The Association of Rebel Youth (AJR), created in 1960, contributed to the National Literacy Campaign by recruiting young instructors and helping with the census of illiterate people. The Pioneers, established in 1961, be-came a selected group of elementary school children. In 1962, the AJR adopted the name Union of Communist Youth (UJC). The UJC went on to become the youth branch of the PCC in 1965, and it still serves that function today with about a half million members (Somos Jovenes Digital, 2009).

The formation of a vanguard party became a contradiction for the Cuban Revolution. The Revolution did not come into power through a vanguard party but rather through the armed rebellion of the July 26 Movement. The Revolution's leftist nationalism later came to embrace socialism at a time when the well developed idea of 'dictatorship of the proletariat' was the standard Marxist alterna-tive to liberal democracy. The theory, created by Marx and Engels, asserts that states exist to protect the capitalist class and private property and that only a revolution leading to a dictatorship of the proletariat can progress to a 'withering away' of the state. The end result, then, would be a classless and stateless communist society in which local communities would make decisions for themselves through popular participation and consensus. Thus, in theory there is a transition from a centralized socialist state to a decentralized organization of society with collectivist values and potential for ad-vanced participatory democracy. Cuba's revolutionary government has experienced the tensions between centralization and decentrali-zation on many levels, and the educational system has been a fine example of this.

From 1961 to 1963, the government took the first small initial steps toward decentralization (Lutjens, 1996). It created provincial bodies called Boards of Coordination, Execution, and Implementation (*Juntas de Coordinación, Ejecución e Implementación* – JUCEIs). The JUCEIs administered national programs at provincial and local levels, but there were problems with personnel and communications. A new system known as Local Power (*Poder Local*) replaced the JUCEIs in 1966. Municipalities elected their local leaders, who facilitated meetings called "Report to the People." These meetings provided forums at which people could express their views. These assemblies ceased by 1968, though, in the wake of a nationwide mobilization, and the Committees in Defense of the Revolution took over the functions that Poder Local had held.

In the late 1960s, the Cuban government took more aggressive measures in transforming the nation. Agrarian reforms culminated in the 1967 transfer of private farms to collectives. In 1968, all remaining private firms were nationalized. A mobilization to harvest 10 million tons of sugar in 1970 neither reached its goal nor propelled the nation's economy as hoped. The government considered new strategies for development in the Revolution with new ideas for education (Kozol, 1978; Franklin, 1997).

The *perfeccionamiento* [improvement] reforms came about in 1971, bringing new trends toward centralization and friendlier relations with the Soviet Union. The First National Congress on Education and Culture convened that year to address problems in the nation's schools such as teacher shortages, lack of materials, poor academic performance, dropouts, mismanagement, disappearing links to communities, and shortcomings in promoting economic and cultural development. These reforms also brought to schools a renewed focus on socialism and the state. Soviet advisors brought pragmatic strategies for educational developments, especially regarding teacher training, higher education and professional development (Lutjens, 1996).

A new governance system called *Poder Popular* [People's Power] emerged on a trial basis in the province of Matanzas in 1974, and it brought a new orientation toward decentralization. The idea of developing professional cadres rather than docile bureaucrats, be-

gun in 1959, received renewed attention. People in Matanzas voted
for their municipal and provincial representatives, and by 1976 all
Cubans were doing so with a new constitution in place. Castro proclaimed that these elections would be different from all previous
ones in Cuba, and they were (Harnecker, 1980). Candidates ran on
their reputations as citizens of their communities without the traditional campaigning that depended on money, sound bites, and public image. Nobody became rich as a politician, and sometimes it
was the poorest person who received a community's nomination
and won an election. Also, a process was in place to have a popular
vote for recalling any representative for any egregious wrongdoing
or neglect.

The effect of People's Power on education was to bring a
greater decentralized accountability, and a detailed account of this
change can be found in Sheryl Lutjen's (1996) book titled *The state,
bureaucracy and the Cuban schools*. The 1976 constitution recognized
education as a right afforded to all children and adults, and it legally reinforced the already *de facto* compulsory education through
ninth grade. There was a new commitment to keep meticulous records on enrollment and on rates of retention, promotion and
graduation. While education for socialism remained important, a
new emphasis on the overall quality of education took root. A new
Ministry of Higher Education became separate from the Ministry
of Education. People's Power established specific functions of provincial and municipal offices of education on the premise that a
decentralized direction would increase the efficiency and effectiveness of schools' instructional and administrative operations. Some
centralized aspects remained, such as national inspectors of curriculum and instruction. The Ministry of Education also created tests
that were administered to all students at the end of sixth, ninth, and
twelfth grades. Still, decentralization at the school level was evident
as a principal shared decision-making power with the participation
of assistant principals, the school council, the union, the Party and
the UJC, and student organizations. The school council, which included parents and members of the community, took a greater role
in the monitoring of school performance after 1976, but the principal continued to be held accountable for outcomes. Although there

were many complaints registered locally by citizens about schools, these were less frequent than complaints to local People's Power regarding other issues. The system of People's Power encouraged citizens to voice their needs and concerns, and schools received more attention from government for making necessary improvements than ever before.

The increase in community involvement in education came about also through the organizing efforts of the Federation of Cuban Women. Their Movement of Militant Mothers for Education (*Movimiento de Madres Combatientes por la Educación*), begun in 1968 with 2,681 members, grew to 430,000 by 1974 and to 1.7 million by 1985 (Lutjens, 1996). The Militant Mothers collaborated as volunteers with schools regarding attendance, retention, promotion, socialist values, civic responsibilities, parent involvement, instructional support, work-study programs, and more. Principals and school councils respected their grassroots efforts and collective voices.

In 1986 another wave of reforms swept into Cuban government, and it was called the 'Rectification Process' (RP). It was announced in February at the Third Congress of the PCC at a critical time for socialism globally, prior to Gorbachev's reforms known as glasnost and perestroika. RP began by addressing 'errors and negative tendencies' in the Cuban Revolution. The government decided to modify some of its programs based on Eastern European models while eliminating others. Castro announced that Cuba's socialism needed to develop better production methods through technology but without adopting capitalist ideology (Azicri, 2000). He mostly was concerned about Cuba's growing trade deficit, and he addressed the need to increase exports while finding ways to curb dependencies on imports. The deficit had brought hardship to social services, with needs for more hospital beds, child-care centers, and urban housing left unmet. There was another concern that people were becoming more inclined to accept individualism while rejecting collectivism and egalitarianism. RP became a movement to return to greater centralization in order to bring national remedies to these national concerns. In its four years of operation it did not solve all of Cuba's problems, but it likely helped the Revolution to survive at a time when socialism was beginning to unravel in Eastern Europe. Education underwent new reforms during RP (Lutjens, 1996). Problems identified in schools were lack of rigor, promotion without due achievement, and teacher turnover. Reform began in February of 1987 with the Eleventh National Seminar for Administrators, Methodologists, and Inspectors. More than 170,000 educators attended, and the outcome was the identification of 410 specific goals. The Twelfth Seminar, held in 1989, determined that 83 percent of these goals had been accomplished. The contributions of the Soviet Union were limited as Cuban educators decidedly moved to the center of the work.

The Cuban Revolution underwent a difficult test when the Soviet Union collapsed. In 1990, Cuba's government declared a "Special Period in Time of Peace" as a response to the economic crisis that resulted from losing the favorable trade conditions with Moscow. To make matters worse, the US tightened the screws of the blockade with the Torricelli-Graham Act of 1992 and the Helms-Burton Act of 1996. The Cuban government created a new Constitution in 1992 and introduced economic reforms that permitted small businesses to operate. Tourism became a kind of necessary evil in its central role for the Revolution's economic recovery. International enterprises formed partnerships with Cuba to build luxurious hotels in Cuba in which only visitors from other countries could afford to stay. Racism was evident when these hotels favored hiring white Cubans for the jobs that involved interactions with foreign tourists. Access to dollars became the source of fortune as waiters made more in tips than doctors could imagine earning in salary. Prostitution made a noticeable return after having been virtually eliminated. In the end, the justification for the increase in tourism was that it became Cuba's leading source of revenue for its funding of education and health care.

Education played a key role in this turning point of the Revolution's history. The survival of socialism in Cuba was at stake, and school curricula continued to uplift Marxism in the context of Martí and Cuban nationalism. A new textbook (Laguna Vila, Martínez Sierra, Mesa Hernández, 1994) for civic education in the

ninth grade contained the following six chapter titles: The Cuban
Family, The Cuban Nation, Work in Socialist Cuba, Socialist Law,
Political Organization of Cuban Society, and Life in Socialist Cuba.
The final chapter summarizes how basic human rights such as education, health care and social security are guaranteed to Cuban
citizens. It highlights how lack of food and medicine has devastated
other countries: "If all of Latin America could have the level of
medical attention that is offered in Cuba, more than 707,000 children would not have died in the year 1988 in the region" (p. 73, as
quoted from del Llano, 1990). It also cites a UNICEF report of
1989 stating that 250,000 children die per week in Third World
nations around the world. With indignation the textbook authors
call these deaths genocide and accuse "capitalism…in the actual
imperialist phase" (p. 73). Later in the chapter more statistics from
UNICEF show how Cuba made remarkable progress from the
1950s to 1992 regarding social indicators of maternal mortality, life
expectancy, literacy, and average educational level.

In 1999, the custody case of the six-year-old Cuban boy Elián
González brought Cuba-US relations into the spotlight of the
global media. An attempt to leave Cuba for Florida ended in a
wrecked boat and the death of Elián's mother. The rescued boy was
delivered to relatives in Miami, but his father in Cuba called for his
return. Massive rallies in Cuba supported the father's efforts. The
first rally, held on December 5, marked the beginning of a new
phase in the course of the Revolution, when there was the coining
of the phrase 'Battle of Ideas' (Kapcia, 2005). Elián returned to his
father, but only after the Clinton Administration authorized armed
officers of the Immigration and Naturalization Service to take the
boy from his Miami relatives.

The Battle of Ideas has continued to be the center of what Cubans see as a new educational revolution (Kapcia, 2005). There
were fears that some of the reforms of the Special Period, like ac-
ceptances of the dollar and self-employment, would lead to a grad-
ual transformation toward capitalism, and it was clear that China
had already become very capitalistic. The Cuban government
forged a new campaign to renew its commitment to socialism and
to national sovereignty independent from global neoliberalism. The

Battle of Ideas linked education with moralism. It re-asserted that Cuba had a moral imperative to struggle against the Spanish empire, against the neocolonial dictatorships that followed, and against the ongoing aggressions of the US blockade and the neoliberal policies of global capitalism. Schools made new efforts to support Cuba's economy with a more pragmatic curriculum for preventing unemployment. New programs emerged for social work, elementary teaching, nursing, cultural education, and technology instruction. At the core of the Battle of Ideas, though, is the ideological appeal to youth for creating a new spirit of community in Cuba while resisting the lures of individualism.

Engagement of youth

Young adults under young leadership fought successfully against Batista's dictatorship, and a massive deployment of mostly adolescents fought successfully against illiteracy in the Literacy Campaign. After those two triumphs, there was the question concerning what would keep youth engaged in the Revolution. The UJC has been the central organization for fostering patriotism in youth for Cuba and the Revolution, and its claimed membership of half a million is an impressive number. Still, several veterans of the Literacy Campaign told me about their concern that young people of the present in Cuba would never truly understand how the Revolution changed the nation and the lives of ordinary people.

The time that *brigadistas* had with their host families in the rural zones was a powerful learning experience. It was mainly landless peasants who fought in the Rebel Army, and they had much to teach the young *brigadistas* in terms of revolutionary spirit and a work ethic for living off of the land. A program called 'Schools to the Countryside' began in the province of Camagüey in 1966 and soon was implemented nation-wide (Fagen, 1969; Lutjens, 1996; Carnoy, 2007). Urban secondary students spent time during school vacations cutting sugar cane and doing other agricultural work. In the 1970s a program called 'Schools in the Countryside' brought urban students to rural boarding schools for a lengthier and more intensive agricultural experience. These schools continued the next two decades with upper secondary students, and they had a positive effect on academic achievement.

Education of youth in Cuba since the Revolution has borrowed progressive elements from Eastern Europe. Cuban pedagogy has been influenced by the child-centered educational philosophies of Russians Lev Vygotski and Anton Makarenko (Carnoy, 2007). The priority for a child-centered education is evident as one teacher works with the same children for their first four years of elementary school so that a single educator can know each student well during this formative time in young lives. Also, a rigorous math curriculum from the German Democratic Republic was translated into Spanish for Cuban schools. It gives a strong foundation for understanding theoretical math concepts, and Cuba continues to use it.

The economic challenges of the Special Period presented difficult situations for many Cuban youth. A university education remained free, but the ability to major in one's chosen field and to find work in it became less promising for many. Low pay, even in the professions, made some college graduates seek menial jobs in tourism, where they could earn substantially more in tips than in their targeted fields. Others lived on the resources of their families, especially when remittances from the US were available. Still, the University of Havana encouraged students to major in the sciences as a way to help the nation advance within the global scientific community.

A survey in 1995 by the weekly journal *Bohemia* showed that a majority of Cuban youth were dissatisfied with their education (Azicri, 2000). Of 171 Havana University students surveyed, more than 80 percent claimed that the teaching they received was deficient. Reasons given for the dissatisfaction were inability to motivate students, instructional rigidity, and too much emphasis on rote memorization. The same survey found that only minorities of students were able to recall completely some of the most important historic events of Cuba, such as the Baraguá Protest led by Antonio Macedo, Martí's death, and the Republic's birth.

A recent study conducted by Martin Carnoy (2007), however, shows that Cuban students outperformed their peers in Brazil and Chile in a standardized test. Carnoy credits these results to Cuba's centralized education system that promotes a high standard of achievement for all students. By contrast, students in Chile and Brazil received widely varying standards of achievement depending on whether they attended a private school, a relatively affluent public school, or a public school in an impoverished area. These inequalities fit with the ideology in both countries that continues to place faith in the market economy. Carnoy emphasized social capital, developed in Cuban families through the nation's egalitarian educational revolution, as the source of Cuba's higher academic performance. Furthermore, he and his graduate assistants from Stanford University found that Cuban teachers were far more likely to use student-centered, constructivist practices than their Brazilian and Chilean counterparts.

Cuban youth gain the benefits of a society that has placed high-quality education as a human right for all. As time removes youth from the triumph of the Revolution in 1959, though, the challenge of keeping them engaged in the ongoing struggles of the Revolution changes. As I wrote in the previous chapter, several of the participants in the Literacy Campaign with whom I spoke mentioned this concern. The Cubans who faced risks and sacrifices in the war and the Campaign contributed directly to the transformation of their nation, but today's youth do not have the same possibilities for playing a role in such historic events. Still, the difficult tests of the Special Period are quite recent, and the Revolution continues to face what Cubans call economic warfare in the ongoing blockade.

Young Cubans continue to be active in international organizations for socialism and other progressive movements. UJC leaders participate in meetings, held about every four years, of the World Federation of Democratic Youth, an anti-imperialist organization founded in London in 1945. The 16th World Festival of Youth and Students was in Venezuela in 2005 with 17,000 participants from 144 countries. Havana will host the Festival for the third time in the summer of 2009 (World Federation of Democratic Youth, 2009).

The UJC also is active with many Cuban organizations in building community at local and national levels. They help to organize national events like the annual celebrations for International Workers' Day every first of May. The young members volunteer regularly with Committees in Defense of the Revolution at events to clean up neighborhoods or to help in planning local festivals. The schools are the social centers for neighborhoods, and communities value the participation of youth in many events and projects. The commitment that neighbors have to local schools was evident when I saw many adults volunteering to do maintenance work on school buildings during the summer vacation. Material resources are scarce due to the blockade, but there is no shortage of a will to volunteer.

Cuban youth are growing up in a society that has been advancing a socialist hegemony for five decades. They have grown up learning that they have a responsibility to participate in constructing socialism. They have not learned to value material affluence but rather a sense of community and egalitarianism.

This is in stark contrast to the rugged individualism that capitalist societies uphold. I recall a time when I was substitute teaching in an urban middle school in the Midwest, and students were gathered in an assembly in the auditorium to hear the assistant principal give a motivational talk. The subject was the relationship between success in school and ability to earn more money. The underlying assumption was that students would go after the carrot of material wealth and consumerism with enough desire to pull them through an otherwise intolerable school experience. More recently, I saw the same motivational strategy with a different tactic in a middle school of a small western town. Each student participated in a simulation that awarded symbolic money in proportion to the individual's grade-point average. The student then visited booths operated by volunteers who tried to sell various goods and services. Again, the message was that performance in school was directly linked to one's ability to consume. Such market-driven socialization is explained well by Samir Amin (2004): "It tends to reduce human beings to the status of 'people' without any identification other than that of being passive 'consumers' in economic life and equally passive 'spectators' (no longer citizens) in political life" (p. 49, Amin's emphases and parenthetical note).

Cuban schools foster citizenship rather than consumerism, and it is a citizenship for national sovereignty and international solidarity. The prospect of contributing one's talents to the development of socialism and participatory democracy is more of an intrinsic motivation. If a Cuban student aspires to become a physician, the motivation comes from a desire to promote health rather than to earn a high salary and status. As I will discuss later, many Cuban physicians have taken their work to parts of the world that have the greatest needs. These professionals, as well as the ones who stay in Cuba, serve people with the satisfaction of contributing to a healthier and happier humanity.

Popular education

In the previous chapter I identified the Literacy Campaign as an example of popular education. Various aspects of popular education continued after the Campaign as Cuban society constructed socialism and promoted participatory democracy. Popular education in capitalist societies is a site of struggle with efforts to raise awareness of institutional and systemic oppressions and to mobilize resistance while promoting alternatives for social and economic justice. In socialist Cuba, popular education is a way of life that is fully supported by the government. Community organizing is not an activity for a few professionals and several dedicated volunteers but rather a process that seeks participation of all ordinary citizens as stakeholders.

Long before the phrase 'popular education' became common, Martí was promoting the idea. In fact, he wrote an essay in 1878 titled "Popular Education." An accurate translation from the Spanish title "Educación Popular" into English would read "Education of the people, by the people, and for the people." In this essay Martí wrote of the potential of increased access to education in the countries of Central America. He also wrote of some examples of effective popular education in France, Germany and Switzerland. Also from this essay comes Martí's (1990a) best known quote: "Knowing how to read is knowing how to walk. Knowing how to write is knowing how to fly" (p. 44).

The Revolution, after its 1959 triumph, wasted no time in giving education a central focus. In addition to planning for the Literacy Campaign, the government launched the "People's University" in 1960. This was a weekly television series involving talks by leaders of the Revolution followed by a question-and-discussion session with a live audience. In 1963 Cuba's Ministry of Foreign Affairs published a 28-page booklet titled *Cuba: A giant school* in English and Spanish. It presents the Revolution as an educational revolution for all Cuban citizens. The idea was that public schools and civil society would blend together to make education a central part of everyday life. This is the essence of popular education – learning creates change, and learning goes beyond the four walls of a school building and beyond the years of formal education.

A case study by Barbara Smith (2008) explores the development of one Cuban non-government organization that has facilitated popular education. The organization's name is Colectivo de Investigación Educativa (CIE), and it was founded in 1995 by Nydia González. Members of its board of directors are leaders from diverse fields and organizations. CIE is among a number of Cuban popular education organizations that sprung from training conferences held in Cuba during the 1980s and 1990s for Latin American popular educators. CIE is inspired by the works of Paulo Freire, and its main purpose "is to support the development of Cuban popular educators and participatory action researchers" (p. 47). The work is performed by volunteers who offer their time beyond what is required for their professional careers. They do not work with a community as leaders but rather "as learners taking advantage of the great wisdom that the community members have to offer them" (p. 47). The nationwide work of CIE has developed into a network for sharing what has been learned in different communities. Procedural topics for community workshops have included "participatory techniques, methodology of popular education, communication, participatory action research, management of projects, systematization, issues of gender, and diagnosis" (p. 61). Some specific topics chosen by communities to explore through popular education methods include neoliberalism, reading promotion, construction of toys, alcoholism, sex education, self-esteem, women, family life, hygiene, herbal medicines, organic agriculture, senior citizens, prostitution, adolescence, food preservation, and children's rights. Some participants earn postgraduate credits in workshops through a course called the Diplomado that is conducted by CIE professors with special training in popular education. Youth from elementary and secondary schools participate in workshops as well through a program called Student CIE. Financial support comes from international organizations that support popular education worldwide, and CIE in turn contributes richly to international workshops.

The work of CIE and other popular education organizations in Cuba provides opportunities for building community and socialist hegemony through participatory democracy. The Italian communist Antonio Gramsci (1971), while imprisoned from 1929 to 1935, developed a theory of hegemony in which the dominant group of society gains popular consent through incentives and messages consistently delivered through compliant agents of civil society such as the media, religious institutions, and schools. This consent is a response to the resulting prestige that the dominant group builds for itself. Gramsci also recognized the role of coercion that states give to armies and police in order to stifle individuals and groups that depart from such consent. He did not work toward ending hegemony but rather toward building a socialist hegemony in place of capitalist hegemony.

A capitalist society, in its interest for maintaining the status quo, does not build popular participation into its hegemony. If people discover that they can change their communities through popular education and direct action, then they might take their power further to demand more of a participatory process in their workplaces through collective bargaining. Demands for living wages, reasonable working conditions, and job security can cut into the bottom-line drive for short-term profits. Corporations exist to make affluent investors more affluent, not to serve the needs and interests of consumers and workers. In the neoliberal world order the option of capital flight to distant lands exists whenever cheaper and more docile (or more violently repressed) labor are available along with low environmental and safety standards. To question this power of neoliberalism is risky for the media, schools, and religious institutions. To be an advocate of community organizing or popular education at the local level is a great challenge considering the pressure from individualism to conform by "sucking it up" whenever problems seem overwhelming. One might act alone to express frustrations to a representative in Congress, to a news editorial, or on an online blog, but to act in concert with a group of concerned citizens is generally not something that people learn to do in school or in their adult lives.

A socialist society such as Cuba's, by contrast, places a high priority on the development of popular participation at various levels – workplace, neighborhood, nation, global community. The Revolution has depended upon the will of ordinary citizens to act together in forming agricultural cooperatives, in mobilizing for the Literacy Campaign, in participating with work councils, in constructing the governance of People's Power, and in embodying international solidarity with medical and educational missions abroad. It is citizenship in an entirely different paradigm from that of the colonial and neocolonial eras before 1959. If any Cuban citizen is not engaged as an agent of change in one's community, then it is not due to lack of opportunity or precedent. Urban and rural workers have a voice with the elected work council of each job site regarding issues of working conditions and discipline, and meetings known as workers' parliaments were instrumental in setting new national economic policies during the Special Period (Harnecker, 1980; Saney, 2004). Representatives of People's Power are ordinary citizens who were elected due to their prior reputations for serving the community and not to influences of money or status. Thus, they are approachable to their constituents in a way that is qualitatively different from elected representatives in a capitalist society with money-driven campaigns. On an international scale Cubans have served in military missions to support African struggles against colonialism and apartheid and have contributed to development of health and education systems in the neediest countries around the world. Although most popular education occurs at the local level, it also by necessity is an important element in creating literacy for critical global citizenship in a neoliberal world order that oppresses the vast majority of humans.

Internationalism and critical global citizenship

The Literacy Campaign, as I have explained, placed a heavy
emphasis on teaching for the understanding of Cuba in historic and
global contexts. As they were learning to read and write for the first
time, illiterate Cubans also were receiving their first structured lessons on the history and cultural geography of their nation and the
world. The Campaign blazed the trail for an internationalism of
critical global citizenship that has set Cuba on a pioneering journey. The nation has looked inward to understand its history of exploitation in colonial and neocolonial eras and to defend its new
direction, but it has also looked outward to take actions of solidarity
in the interests of social and economic justice for the people of other
Latin American nations and throughout the entire Third World.

Cuban internationalism has involved sacrifice including loss of
lives in foreign wars. Piero Gleijeses (2002) wrote of how the Cuban
government supported different armed struggles in Africa from
1959 to 1976. Cuban troops fought as early as 1963 to defend Algeria's independence against Moroccan aggression and as late as 1976
to keep Angola out of the hands of UNITA rebels, who under
South African influence likely would have formed a similar regime
of racist apartheid. These deployments at times involved fighting
reactionary forces that were supported quietly by the US. At times
they also went forward against the advice of the Soviet Union. Not
all of Cuba's military interventions in Africa were successful, but
they confirmed to the world that the small Caribbean nation was
willing to fight on behalf of struggles in other nations for sovereignty and social justice. Nelson Mandela's ongoing friendship with
Fidel Castro is a testimony to the gratitude that many African
movements have had for Cuban contributions.

An emphasis on science education has resulted in a strong supply of physicians, and Cuba's medical missions to countries with the
greatest needs have been another expression of international solidarity. Health care in Cuba has risen to social indicators that are
comparable to First World countries, but the Cuban medical community sees its commitment as extending to underdeveloped countries around the world. Julie Feinsilver (2003) calls this policy

"medical diplomacy." Since Cuba's medical assistance to Third
World countries began with Algeria in 1963, dozens of countries
have received long-term aid while many others have received tem-
porary aid in emergency situations. Additionally, Cuba's Latin
American School of Medicine provides free tuition to students from
low-income families throughout Latin America and the US.
Graduates in 2007 included the first eight US citizens to complete
the program. They, like all graduates of the school, made a pledge
to work in zones with the greatest needs for medical care. All of this
work in health development has bolstered Cuba's image as a be-
nevolent nation that is extraordinarily generous despite its own
economic limitations.

Cuba also has provided teachers to assist developing nations
with their literacy campaigns. Nicaragua's National Literacy Campaign of 1980 under the revolutionary Sandinista government received the support of many Cuban teachers, some of whom were
veterans of Cuba's Campaign. Since then, Cuba has developed a
literacy program called *Yo Sí Puedo* [Yes, I Can] with successful results in more than 15 countries and international recognition in an
award from UNESCO (2006). Some of the most recent national
literacy campaigns to apply *Yo Sí Puedo* have been in Haiti, Venezuela, Bolivia, Ecuador, Paraguay, and East Timor. This method
excludes the political content that appeared in Cuba's Campaign in
order to facilitate international application without controversy. It
utilizes electronic technology in conjunction with face-to-face classroom instruction in order to maximize results with optimal cost-
effectiveness.

Perhaps Cuba's greatest contribution to internationalism is its
example of connecting political economy with national sovereignty.
Diana Raby (2009) argues that the Cuban Revolution still matters
in today's world because of this connection and how it is being realized in other Latin American countries. Many Latin American nations recently have elected presidents and legislative bodies that are
left of center. Three of these governments in particular – those of
Venezuela, Bolivia, and Ecuador – have declared a direction toward socialism and away from dependence on the neoliberal mandates attached to loans from the World Bank and the IMF. Para-

guay more recently has elected a president with a similar orientation but presently not with the support of the other branches of government. Raby states that Cuba's Revolution has made it possible for these South American countries to see and, in their own unique ways, to follow an example of sustained resistance against US hegemony and global capitalism. She sees a pattern in which the more recent of these national transformations have been more democratic from their inceptions. This is not to condemn Cuba and Venezuela but rather to acknowledge that the boldness of Cuba's armed Revolution influenced Venezuela with Chavez's 1992 coup attempt and his subsequent rise to power through elections, which in turn encouraged voters of Bolivia, Ecuador, and Paraguay to choose presidential candidates who reject the neoliberal paradigm. Raby thus concludes, "Without Cuba, then no Venezuela; and without Venezuela, no Bolivia, no Ecuador, and no Paraguay, and no revival (however imperfect) of Sandinista Nicaragua" (p. 11, Raby's parenthetic note). Cuba still bears the brunt of the punishment with the ongoing blockade by the US, but there appears to be no stopping other nations in Latin America as they defiantly chart their own courses.

Elena Díaz González (2005), a Cuban economist, has explained four ways that Cuban policy has differed sharply from neoliberalism. First, she cites UN figures showing that world-wide poverty has increased in the neoliberal era: "The income difference between the richest and poorest one-fifth of the world population was 30 to 1 in 1960, 60 to 1 in 1990 and 74 to 1 in 1997" (p. 265, as cited from United Nations Development Program). Díaz Gonzalez argues that neoliberalism, because it increases poverty, also increases social polarization and social exclusion. Cuba, by contrast, has developed policies for taxes and regulations to prevent income polarization and severe poverty. Second, Cuba rejects neoliberalism's position on the continuum of social exclusion and solidarity. Under neoliberalism there is pressure for underdeveloped countries to privatize services such as education, health care and elderly pensions, which results in less access for economically distressed families. Women and children suffer the most. Cuba's sense of ethics demands that not one person be abandoned, and the government ensures univer-

sal education, health care, and social security. Third, Cuba con-
trasts with neoliberalism on the continuum of social fragmentation
versus social participation. Neoliberalism has caused a polarization
in labor resulting in a highly skilled elite and a growing population
of disenfranchised workers who often must survive in an informal
economy. A massive deskilling process ensures that there will be a
large global pool of laborers who out of desperation will accept jobs
that are low in standards for pay, safety and security. Cuba, on the
other hand, prioritizes full employment and training for all in need
of skills, and workers play an important role in public-policymaking
through their representation in the Cuban Confederation of Workers. Fourth and finally, Cuba fundamentally rejects neoliberalism's
treatment of ideology as a commodity. Neoliberal control of the
media has resulted in a world where individualism and selfishness
become virtues. All people of all cultures are led to believe that the
US model of consumption, as revealed in movies, videos and advertisements, is available to all. Messages of human spirituality and
values of indigenous cultures are silenced or destroyed, and access
to the Internet is denied to people living in poverty. The Cuban
Revolution, though, has identified its central value as solidarity
among people. It confronts neoliberal ideology in the Battle of
Ideas. It also strives to make televisions and computers more available to schools, homes and communities.

Concluding thoughts

Cuba's National Literacy Campaign of 1961 was a historical
turning point for Cuba and the entire world. The revolutionary
government declared that illiteracy was a social and political crime
perpetuated by centuries of Spanish colonialism and decades of US
neocolonialism. It placed the Campaign high in its immediate priorities to ensure that the Revolution would indeed be revolutionary
and sustainable. Popular participation has been at the center of the
ethical essence of the Revolution, and only an educated populace
can participate in a meaningful way. As I have addressed, the
Campaign had important national antecedents for the idea of uni-

versal literacy and has had a powerful legacy in Cuba and in the world.

My lens of critical global citizenship for viewing the Campaign takes into view this wide scope of history and legacy. A transformative event such as the Campaign does not occur because a charismatic leader suddenly ordains it, nor does it blossom immediately without the right seed being planted in the right place and the right time. The idea of literacy as a human right has developed through a series of struggles in Cuba and elsewhere. In Cuba it nearly germinated with the Ten Years War of 1868 to 1878 in the fight for national sovereignty and the abolition of slavery. Martí then kept the idea alive within his revolutionary anti-imperialism, but the neocolonial outcome of the new Cuban republic ensured that mass illiteracy would continue. The seed might have settled after a popular movement ousted the Machado dictatorship, but Batista moved in to become the *de facto*, and later *de jure*, US-supported dictator in his place. It was not until the triumph of the Revolution in 1959 that the idea could take root and grow. The Year of Education, 1961, saw the Campaign survive even through the storm that was the Bay of Pigs invasion. Still, this was only the beginning since newly literate Cubans had only a first-grade level of reading and writing. Most continued their studies, and education for all Cubans became the food that helped the tree of the Revolution grow fully.

The Cuban Revolution triumphed through an armed struggle, but it has been able to survive the US blockade and the Special Period only because of its substance created by universal education. Education as a process and schools as institutions reflect the norms and values of the greater society, and only a revolution can bring revolutionary education. At the same time, only a revolutionary education can sustain a revolution. Cuba has lived that reality for 50 years, and the Bolivarian Revolution of Venezuela, having completed its national literacy campaign called Misión Robinson, is still working through its early stages to find its own path. Likewise, Bolivia and Ecuador have made grand commitments to national literacy campaigns and new directions against the neoliberal tide. The possibilities for revolutionary change in these countries are real as they are using the weapon of education to struggle for a new and authentic sovereignty that upholds social justice and human dignity.

What can critical educators of countries not in a revolutionary process do? I can only comment on my experience of having been in a cohort of 17 doctoral students in a program of critical pedagogy (now sadly defunct) at a university in the US from 2000 to 2004. We all were striving to understand the oppressions of racism, sexism, heterosexism, classism, and able-ism in order to become more effective agents of change in our educational professions. There were many moments of tension in which we debated over which oppression was the worst. In the end we matured in our understandings and realized that all oppressions are terribly dehumanizing and that we need each other as allies to combat all of them. Five years have passed, and I have lost touch with everyone in the cohort except for the only other person who did dissertation work in Cuba. Still, I know that each cohort member made me think, rethink, and sometimes change my views on education and the world. I never had allies like them in the large urban high school in which I was teaching during the same years and beyond, but then there never was an opportunity (or at that stage I was not ready to see or create an opportunity) in such a school to study and discuss matters of oppression and resistance in a deep way with any of my teaching colleagues.

I recall a moment in one doctoral course in which a cohort member asked the professor whether one needs to be revolutionary in order to be in critical pedagogy. I cannot remember the professor's response, but that question made me think and does so still. If I could return to that classroom moment, I would comment that revolutionary times require revolutionary thinking and action. Then I would pose the question, "Are we now in revolutionary times?" That is not a rhetorical question but rather one that must be debated openly among critical educators.

I argue that, yes, we are in revolutionary times. Neoliberalism has brought the world to a pre-revolutionary condition that rewards some immensely while leaving the majority of humanity struggling to cope with uncertainty, including nearly a billion people struggling to survive (United Nations World Food Program, 2009). It is

the global policy of unfettered capitalism, supported by global finance, the uncritical and handsomely rewarded corporate media,
and the mighty military of the US. Neoliberalism is fundamentally
inhumane, undemocratic, and unsustainable (Jensen, 2007). It sorts
out and polarizes winners and losers globally, devastating vast regions and entire indigenous cultures in the dog-eat-dog, sink-or-
swim, lop-sided contest for luxury or misery. Women, children, the
elderly, and people of color suffer at disproportionately higher
rates, as they did during prior eras of colonialism. International
trade agreements become policy behind closed doors where only a
few ordained members of the global oligarchy can have a voice and
a vote. The false promise is that all people in the world can work
hard and not only move their families into better living conditions
but also become like upper-middle-class US consumers, and this is
utterly unsustainable in our world of finite resources and impending
climate change.

What can be done among educators who are willing to do the
research and uncover the pre-revolutionary condition of neoliberalism? First, one must do the research. Data from the UN and many
'alternative' sources like United for a Fair Economy and Global
Exchange reveal just how unjust the world's top-down economic
model is. Next, critical educators against the neoliberal world order
must find, challenge, and support each other. Nobody can do this
work alone. While I was teaching social studies in high school, the
school nurse became the only person with whom I could share my
deepest concerns and hopes about students, education and our
troubled world. Without her, the frequent and aimless complaining
episodes of liberal teachers would not have been enough to sustain
my morale. Finally, partners and groups of committed educators
must keep hope and action alive. Our local communities and the
world urgently need us to develop praxis against neoliberalism and
for a more democratic, sustainable and humane political economy.
Critical educators can and must develop a popular education for
such transformation in spite of the narrow scope of standards that
states require to be taught.

This kind of popular education has no limit in participation and
possibilities. Narrow, incremental school reform can become a blos-

soming community for progressive and even radical change, involving students, teachers, families, and the tax-paying citizens. A valuable project can be an exploration into how planting an urban garden and supporting farmers' markets instead of multinational big-box chains can build community while keeping money and resources within the community. Another project on a more global scale could be an investigation into where commodities like clothing are made, how they are made, to whom go what profits, and whether such production is humane and sustainable. Both of these projects ultimately make all participants think about the consequences of their choices as consumers. If done with sufficient time, resources, and intention, they can be powerful experiences for developing a lifelong critical global citizenship.

Finally, I must return to Cuba's National Literacy Campaign. Cuba won its Revolutionary War with the Rebel Army and immediately put into place a plan for a mass movement of rebel literacy that could sustain the Revolution's goals for national sovereignty and social justice. Today, there are critical educators around the world with the courage to challenge neoliberalism and the vision to know that a better world is possible through peaceful and determined struggle. We can benefit from the knowledge of the revolutionary educational achievements of Cuba. Youth everywhere can be inspired by what Cuban youth did in the Campaign. People of all ages and walks of life can be inspired by the popular education and elements of participatory democracy occurring in Cuba. Finally, people around the world can be moved to pressure the US government to end the blockade and to let Cuba live in peace. This is a worthy project for critical global citizens.

Bibliography

Abendroth, M. G. (2005). *Cuba's national literacy campaign: A mass movement of emancipatory global civic education* (Unpublished doctoral dissertation). St. Paul: University of St. Thomas.

Amin, S. (2004). *The liberal virus: Permanent war and the Americanization of the world* (J. H. Membrez, Trans). New York: Monthly Review Press.

Anyon, J. (1980). Social class and the hidden curriculum of work. *Journal of Education, 162*(1), 67-92.

Azicri, M. (2000). *Cuba today and tomorrow: Reinventing socialism.* Gainesville, FL: University Press of Florida.

Becker, M. (2003). *Mariátegui and the problem of race in Latin America* (Unpublished paper). Kirksville, MO: Truman State University.

Benjamin, M., Collins, J., & Scott, M. (2003). The agrarian revolution. In Chomsky, A., Carr, B, & Smorkaloff, P. M. (Eds.). *The Cuba reader: History, culture, politics.* Durham: Duke University Press.

Cabral, A. (1970). *Revolution in Guinea: Selected texts* (R. Handyside, Trans.). New York: Monthly Review Press.

Canfux, J. (1981). A brief description of the "Battle for the Sixth Grade." *Journal of Reading, 25*(3), 226-233.

Carnoy, M. (2007). *Cuba's academic advantage: Why students in Cuba do better in school.* Stanford, CA: Stanford University Press.

Castro, F. (1961). Saluda el Dr. Fidel Castro a los maestros revolucionarios y rinde tributo a un martir [Dr. Fidel Castro salutes revolutionary teachers and pays homage to a martyr]. *Obra Revolucionaria*(5), 23-36.

Castro, F. (1968). *History will absolve me: The Moncada trial defence speech, Santiago de Cuba, October 16th, 1953.* London: Jonathan Cape.

Chomsky, A., Carr, B, & Smorkaloff, P. M. (Eds.). (2003). *The Cuba reader: History, culture, politics.* Durham: Duke University Press.

Chu, D. (1980). *Chairman Mao: Education of the proletariat.* New York: Philosophical Library.

Comisión Nacional de Alfabetización. (1961a). *Alfabeticemos* [Let's teach literacy]. Havana: Imprenta Nacional de Cuba.

Comisión Nacional de Alfabetización. (1961b). *¡Venceremos!* [We will triumph!]. Havana: Imprenta Nacional de Cuba.

Comisión Nacional de Alfabetización. (1961c). *Arma Nueva, 2*(1). Havana: Impenta Nacional de Cuba.

Comisión Nacional de Alfabetización. (1961d). *Cumpliremos.* Havana: Imprenta Nacional de Cuba.

Comisión Nacional de Alfabetización. (1961e). *Segundo Congreso de Consejos Municipales de Educación* [Second Congress of the Municipal Councils of Education]. (1961). Havana: Imprenta Nacional de Cuba.

Comisión Nacional de Alfabetización y Educación Fundamental, & Casa de las Américas. (1961). *La Cartilla ¡Venceremos!: Antecedentes* [The primer 'We will triumph!': Antecedents]. Havana: Imprenta Nacional de Cuba.

DeFronzo, J. (2007). *Revolutions and revolutionary movements* (3rd ed.). Boulder: Westview Press.

Del Llano, E. (1990). Defender la vida [Defending life]. *Trabajadores,* March 9, 4.

Díaz González, E. (2005). Is the socialist model still a viable alternative for Cuba? In Bell Lara, J. & Dello Buono, R. A.

(Eds.). *Cuba in the 21st Century: Realities and perspectives* (R. A. Dello Buono, Trans.). Havana: Editorial José Martí.

Escalante, F. (1995). In Muñiz, M. (Ed.), *The Secret War: CIA covert operations against Cuba, 1959-1962* (M. Shaw, Trans.). Melbourne: Ocean Press.

Estenoz, E. (2003). The Independent Party of Color. In Chomsky, A., Carr, B, & Smorkaloff, P. M. (Eds.). *The Cuba reader: History, culture, politics*. Durham: Duke University Press.

Fagen, R. R. (1969). *The transformation of political culture in Cuba*. Stanford, CA: Stanford University Press.

Fanon, F. (1963). *The wretched of the earth* (C. Farrington, Trans.). New York: Grove Press.

Farber, S. (1976). *Revolution and reaction in Cuba: A political sociology from Machado to Castro*. Middletown, CT: Wesleyan University Press.

Farber, S. (2006). *The origins of the Cuban Revolution reconsidered*. Chapel Hill: University of North Carolina Press.

Feinsilver, J. (2003). Cuban medical diplomacy. In Chomsky, A., Carr, B, & Smorkaloff, P. M. (Eds.). *The Cuba reader: History, culture, politics*. Durham: Duke University Press.

Ferrer, R. (1961). La Ley de Nacionalización de la Enseñanza [The Nationalization of Education Law]. *Cuba Socialista, 1*(1), 47-65.

Foreign Policy Association, Inc. (1935), *Problems of the new Cuba: Report of the Commission on Cuban Affairs*. New York: Foreign Policy Association, Inc.

Franklin, J. (1997). *Cuba and the United States: A chronological history*. Melbourne: Ocean Press.

Gleijeses, P. (2002). *Conflicting missions: Havana, Washington, and Africa, 1959-1976*. Chapel Hill: University of North Carolina Press.

Gott, R. (2004). *Cuba: A new history.* New Haven: Yale Press.

Gramsci, A. (1971). Problems of history and culture (Q. Hoare & G. N. Smith, Trans.). In Q. Hoare & G. N. Smith (Eds.), *Selections from the prison notebooks.* New York: International Publishers.

Guevara, E. (1968). *Reminiscences of the Cuban Revolutionary War.* New York: Monthly Review Press.

Guevara, E. (2003). Social ideals of the Rebel Army. In Deutchmann, D. (Ed.). *Che Guevara reader: Writings on politics and revolution* (2nd ed.). Melbourne: Ocean Press.

Guevara, E. (2003). Socialism and man in Cuba. In Deutchmann, D. (Ed.). *Che Guevara reader: Writings on politics and revolution* (2nd Ed.). Melbourne: Ocean Press.

Harnecker, M. (Ed.). (1980). *Cuba: Dictatorship or democracy?* (5th ed.), (P. Greanville, Trans.). Westport, CT: Lawrence Hill & Company.

Hart, A. (2004). *Aldabonazo: Inside the Cuban revolutionary underground, 1952-1958.* New York: Pathfinder.

Hawkins, J. N. (1974). *Mao Tse-Tung and education: His thoughts and teachings.* Hamden, CT: The Shoe String Press, Inc.

Helg, A. (1995). *Our rightful share: The Afro-Cuban struggle for equality, 1886-1912.* Chapel Hill, NC: University of North Carolina Press.

Jensen, R. (2007). *Anti-capitalism in five minutes or less.* Retrieved June 9, 2009, from http://www.commondreams.org/archive/2007/04/30/865.

Johnson, J. J. (2003). U.S. cartoonists portray Cuba. In Chomsky, A., Carr, B, & Smorkaloff, P. M. (Eds.). *The Cuba reader: History, culture, politics.* Durham: Duke University Press.

Judson, C. F. (1984). *Cuba and the revolutionary myth: The political education of the Cuban rebel army, 1953-1963*. Boulder, CO: Westview Press.

Kapcia, A. (2005). Educational revolution and revolutionary morality in Cuba: The 'New Man', youth and the new 'Battle of Ideas'. *Journal of Moral Education, (34)*4, 399-412.

Keeble, A., Ed. (2001). *In the spirit of wandering teachers: Cuban Literacy Campaign, 1961*. Melbourne: Ocean Press.

Kerka, S. (1997). *Popular education: Adult education for social change*. Retrieved February 14, 2009, from http://www.ericdigests.org/1998-1/popular.htm.

Kirk, J. M. (1983). *José Martí: Mentor of the Cuban nation*. Tampa: University Presses of Florida.

Klein, N. (2007). *The shock doctrine: The rise of disaster capitalism*. New York: Metropolitan Books.

Kozol, J. (1978). A new look at the literacy campaign in Cuba. *Harvard Educational Review, 48*(3), 341-377.

Kumanev, V. (1970). Lenin's principles of abolishing illiteracy and their implementation in the USSR. *Problems of the contemporary world, 1*(3), 163-183.

Laguna Vila, D., Martínez Sierra, L., Mesa Hernández, H. A., Herrera Orúe, E., & Rodríguez Ben, J. (1994). *Educación cívica: Noveno grado* [Civic education: Ninth grade]. Havana: Editorial Pueblo y Educación.

Lorenzetto, A., & Neys, K. (1965). *Methods and means utilized in Cuba to eliminate illiteracy*. Havana: Cuban National Commission for Unesco.

Lutjens, S. L. (1996). *The state, bureaucracy, and the Cuban schools: power and participation*. Boulder, CO: Westview Press.

MacDonald, T. (1985). *Making a new people: Education in revolutionary Cuba*. Vancouver: New Star.

Mariátegui, J. C. (1971). *Seven essays of interpretation of Peruvian reality* (M. Urquidi, Trans.). Austin: University of Texas Press.

Marx, K. (1906). *Capital: A critique of political economy* (S. Moore & E. Aveling, Trans., from 3rd German Edition). New York: The Modern Library.

Martí, J. (1990a). Educación popular [Popular education]. In E. López Ugarte (Ed.), *Ideario pedagógico* [Pedagogical designs] (pp. 49-52). Havana: Centro de Estudios Martianos.

Martí, J. (1990b). Maestros ambulantes [Traveling teachers]. In E. López Ugarte (Ed.), *Ideario pedagógico* [Pedagogical designs] (pp. 49-52). Havana: Centro de Estudios Martianos.

Martí, J. (1999). Nuestra América [Our America]. In D. Shnookal & M. Muñiz (Eds.), *José Martí reader: Writings on the Americas*. New York: Ocean Press.

McGee Deutsch, S. (1999). *Las derechas: The extreme right in Argentina, Brazil and Chile, 1890-1939*. Stanford, CA: Standford University Press.

McLaren, P. (2000). *Che Guevara, Paulo Freire, and the pedagogy of revolution*. Lanham, MD: Rowman & Littlefield.

Medical Students for Cuba. (2006). *Summary report of American Association of World Health on impact of US embargo on health of Cuban people*. Retrieved September 12, 2008, from http://www-personal.umich.edu/ ~alcheng/cuba06/FoodMedicine.html.

Mella, J. A. (1975). *J. A. Mella: Documentos y Artículos* [Documents and Articles]. Havana: Editorial de Ciencias Sociales.

Ministry of Foreign Affairs. (1963). *Cuba: A giant school*. Havana.

Murillo, J., Vigo, E., Torres, V., Romani, G., & Beltran, R. (1964). *Cinco maestro argentinos alfabetizaron en Cuba* [Five Argentine teachers taught literacy in Cuba]. Havana: Ediciones "Hoy en la Cultura."

Niu, X. (1994). *Education east and west: The influence of Mao Zedong and John Dewey.* San Francisco: International Scholars Publications.

Ordóñez Careller, C. (1995). *La salud pública en Cuba: Experiencias de un trabajador de la salud* [Public health in Cuba: Experiences of a health worker]. Havana: Impreso en el Palacio de las Convenciones.

Parenti, M. (2004). *Superpatriotism.* San Francisco: City Lights Books.

Pérez, L. A., Jr. (2008). *Cuba in the American imagination: Metaphor and the imperial ethos.* Chapel Hill: University of North Carolina Press.

Pérez Cruz, F. d. J. (2001). *La alfabetización en Cuba: Lectura histórica para pensar el presente* [Literacy in Cuba: Historical reading to consider the present]. Havana: Editorial de Ciencias Sociales.

Ponce, A. (1975). Educación y lucha de clases [Education and class struggle]. In J. Marinello (Ed.), *Obras.* Havana: Casa de las Américas.

Quiroz, A. W. (2001). La reforma educacional en Cuba, 1898-1909 [Educational reform in Cuba]. In Hernández R. & Coatsworth, J. H. (Eds.). *Culturas encontradas: Cuba y los Estados Unidos* [Colliding cultures: Cuba and the United States]. La Habana: Centro de Investigación y Desarrollo de la Cultura Cubana Juan Marinello. Cambridge: Harvard University Press.

Raby, D. (2009). Why Cuba still matters. *Monthly Review (60)*8, 1-13.

Roman, P. (2003). *People's power: Cuba's experience with representative government* (Updated Ed.). Lanham, MD: Rowman & Littlefield Publishers, Inc.

Saney, I. (2004). *Cuba: A revolution in motion.* New York: Zed Books Ltd.

Select Committee to Study Governmental Operations with Respect to Intelligence Activities. (2003). The assassination plots. In Chomsky, A., Carr, B, & Smorkaloff, P. M. (Eds.). *The Cuba reader: History, culture, politics.* Durham: Duke University Press.

Sleeter, C. (2004). *Standardizing imperialism.* Retrieved September 13, 2008, from http://www.rethinkingschools.org/archive/19_01/impe 191.shtml.

Smith, B. (2008). *Cuban popular education: One descriptive case study.* (Unpublished doctoral dissertation). St. Paul: University of St. Thomas.

Somos Jovenes Digital. (2009). *Unión de Jovenes Comunistas* [Union of Young Communists]. Retrieved April 22, 2009, from http://www.somosjovenes.cu/ index/semana10/jovcomunist.htm

Stromquist, N. (2002). *Education in a globalized world: The connectivity of power, technology, and knowledge.* Lanham, MD: Rowman & Littlefield Publishers, Inc.

Suchlicki, J. (1969). *University students and revolution in Cuba, 1920-1968.* Coral Gables, FL: University of Miami Press.

Torroella, G. (1959). Veinte y cinco preguntas al Dr. Armando Hart, Ministro de Educación [Twenty-three questions to Dr. Armando Hart, Minister of Education]. *Bohemia, 51*(8), 38-41, 138.

Turner Martí, L. (1999). *Del pensamiento pedagógico de Ernesto Che Guevara* [Of the pedagogical thinking of Ernesto Che Guevara]. Havana: Editorial Capitán San Luis.

UNESCO. (2006). *UNESCO International Reading Association Literacy Prize.* Retrieved June 7, 2009, from http://unesdoc.unesco.org/images/0014/001484/148481 e.pdf.

United Nations World Food Program. (2009). *Who are the hungry?* Retrieved   June   17,   2009,   from http://www.wfp.org/hunger/who-are.

White, C., & Openshaw R. (2004). *Democracy at the crossroads: International perspectives on critical global citizenship education.* Lanham, MD: Lexington Books.

White, T. (1898). *Pictoral history of our war with Spain for Cuba's freedom.* Freedom Publishing Co.

Wolf, E. R. (1969). *Peasant wars of the twentieth century.* New York: Harper & Row.

World Federation of Democratic Youth. (2009). *Festivals.* Retrieved May 24, 2009, from http://www.wfdy.org/festivals/.

Zinn, H. (2001). *A people's history of the United States: 1492-present* (Revised and updated ed.). New York: HarperPerennial.

Index

Roosevelt, Theodore, 35
Royal Economic Society of
  Friends of the Nation, 25
Ruis, Alfreda Marques, 101
Russia, 38, 57-58, 60, 64
  see also Soviet Union

Saco, José Antonio, 27
Saladrigas, Carlos, 42
Sandinista National Liberation
  Front (Sandinistas), 16, 63, 142
  see also Nicaragua
Sandino, Augusto César, 63
Santana, Ricardo, 84-85
Sartre, Jean-Paul, 65
School of Medical Sciences, see
  Latin American School of
  Medicine
schools, nationalization of, 83,
  112, 124
Schools of Revolutionary Instruc-
  tion (EIR), 124
"Schools of the Countryside," 124,
  133
Second Congress of Municipal
  Councils of Education, 84-85,
  91
Second War of Independence, 7,
  18-19, 23, 31
Seminar for Administrators,
  Methodologists, and Inspectors,
  131
Smathers, George, 54
Socialist Party of Cuba, 38
Solana, Gladys Hernández, 114
"Soles y Rayos de Bolívar, " 26
Soviet Union, 9-10, 14, 42, 49, 56-
  57, 64, 65-66, 124, 128, 131
  see also "Special Period"
Spain, 1, 6-7, 23-29, 32-33, 54, 60
Spanish-American War, 33
"Special Period," xxvi, 10, 14,
  131-135, 140
sugar (industry), 27, 36, 37-38, 42,
  54, 55, 64, 65

nationalization of, 40, 44, 53,
  71, 128
U.S. boycott of, 57

Taft, William Howard, 35
Ten Years War, 29, 145
tourism (industry), 10, 14, 131,
  134
Torricelli-Graham Act, 10, 131
Treaty of Paris, 33
Trudeau, Pierre Elliot, xi-xii
Trujillo, Leonidas, 64-65
Truman Administration, 43
Twain, Mark, 33

Union of Communist Youth
  (UJC), 127, 133, 135
UNITA, 4, 141
United Nations, 5
  Development Program, 143
  World Food Program, 146
United Nations Educational,
  Scienctific and Cultural Orga-
  nization (UNESCO), 4, 113,
  142
United Party of the Socialist Revo-
  lution, see Communist Party of
  Cuba (PCC)
University of Saint Thomas, ix-x,
  71
Urgent Plan of Cuban Literacy,
  51
Urrutia, Manuel, 50, 54

Varela, Félix, 12, 26-27
Varona, Enrique José, 35-36
¡Venceremos! (textbook), 68, 75-78
Venceremos Brigade, 11
Venezuela, 4, 17, 118, 143
Misión Robinson (National Literacy
  Campaign), 99, 103, 113, 145
resistance to neoliberalism, 11, 17
see also Organic Education Act
Villazón, Osvaldo Hernández, 98
Vygotski, Lev, 134

About the Author

Mark Abendroth is assistant professor of social studies education at the Long Island Center of Empire State College, a SUNY institution for age-diverse students throughout the State of New York. This is his first book, and he has other published writings on critical global citizenship and education. His other research interests include immigrants' cultural identities in schools and the political economy of education. He lives with his wife in Hauppauge, New York.

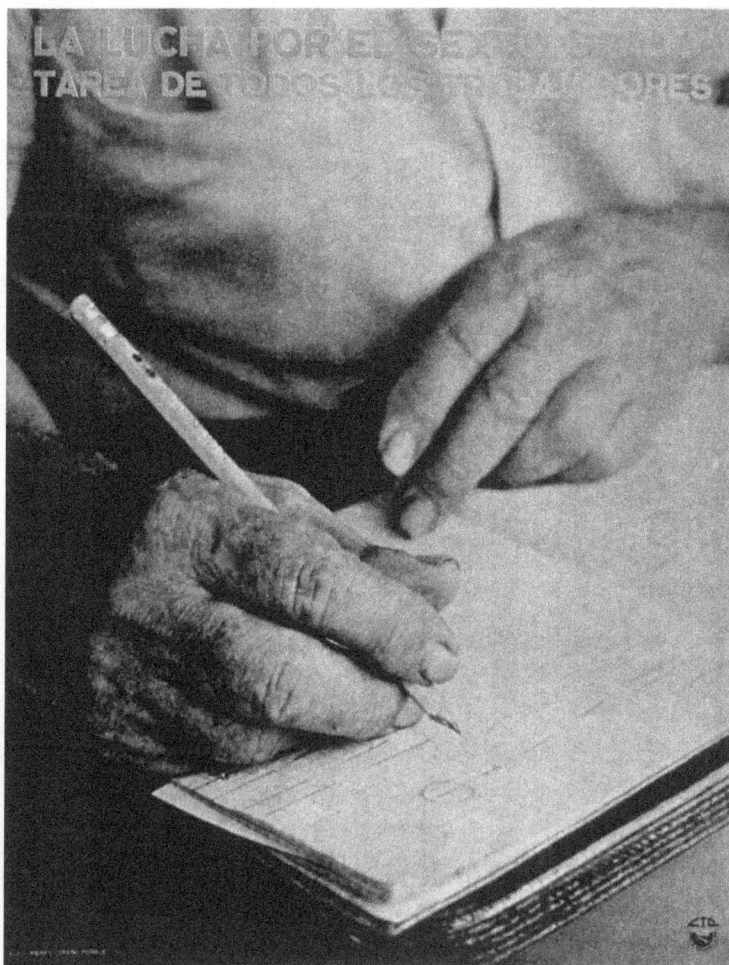

La lucha por el sexto grado : Tarea de todos los trabajadores
("The challenge to complete the sixth grade - an assignment for all workers."). Eduardo Marín Potrillé. Cuban Workers Confederation (CTC).
Published by Editora Politica, 1976.

Image courtesy of Lincoln Cushing / Docs Populi.